LONDON TRANSPORT

BUSES & COACHES

1954

LONDON TRANSPORT

BUSES & COACHES

1954

John A.S. Hambley

Published in 1994 by
IMAGES

in conjunction with
JOHN A. S. HAMBLEY
7 Linden Road,
Dunstable,
Beds. LU5 4NZ

Additional text and research by David A. Ruddom.

British Library Cataloguing in Publication Data
A catalogue record for this book is available from the British Library

ISBN 1 897817 45 2

Front cover photograph:
Standing outside Broad Street Station nicely presented RTW382 operates as D24 on route 11, while behind RTW115 operates on the same route. It should be pointed out that hand signals were still the order of the day, the trafficator arm niche being panelled over and flashing elephant ears were still on the drawing board. (J.H. Aston)

Back cover photograph:
K424 an AEC bus built in 1920 with LGOC 46 seat bodywork is parked in Waterloo Place at the end of the Omnibus Society Silver Jubilee run on the 25th September. The procession of buses included the K, S, B and NS from the London Transport Collection and also the 1908 Daimler replica of Barton Transport driven by Mr. T.A. Barton with Mrs. Barton who can just be seen in this picture. The special side advertisements were prepared by Mr. John Birch of Birch Brothers and were actually fixed on with Vaseline so as not to damage the vehicles. The organisers were thankful it was not a windy day! (J.C. Gillham)

Designed and produced by Images (Publishing) Malvern Ltd.
Printed and bound by Wincanton Print, Wincanton, Somerset.

TD54 shows to good advantage the recessed first panel to the nearside, being an identical body shell to that used on T769 to T798 which had a sliding door fitted. This second batch of TDs had bodywork built by Mann Egerton and were classified 1/1TD2. The bus stands outside Edgware garage blinded for a short working on route 240A which eventually became the last route to operate this class. (Lens of Sutton)

Acknowledgements

I should like to thank the following for use of their photographic material in this book: James H Aston, M. Banks, Ronald G Bristow, Bob Burrell, C. Carter, Alan B Cross, John Fozard, John Gascoine, J.C. Gillham, Peter Gomm, Peter Gulland, Roy Hobbs, Roger Holmes, D.A. Jones, D.W.K. Jones, Kevin Lane, W.R. Legg, London Trolleybus Preservation Society, Roy Ludgate, Ian Maclean, Roy Marshall, Gerald Mead, J.H. Meredith, Geoff Morant, M.R.M. New, J.H. Price, Norman Rayfield, Michael Rooum, David A. Ruddom, G.A. Rixon, Sabena Belgian World Airlines, R.H.G. Simpson, John Smith of Lens of Sutton, John G.S. Smith, and Sheila Taylor of the London Transport Museum.

Once again a number of photographs have been used which carry no identification of their origins. I am always pleased to acknowledge ownership of prints in later volumes and should be grateful if any custodians of such items would contact me.

Much use has again been made of the various publications produced by the PSV Circle over the years dealing with the vehicles. For route information reference has been made to the many publications produced by LOTS and the Omnibus Society. Thanks are therefore extended to all these organisations. 1954 has been the first volume in this series in which RTs and RFs have become universal throughout most of the LT system and I would also like to acknowledge assistance from the RT/RF Register. This preservation group is open to all and not only to vehicle owners and enquiries should be made to 96 Carlton Crescent, Luton, LU3 1EW. Once again David Ruddom must be singled out for all the time and help given me in bringing this book to fruition. Much greatly appreciated help and patience has been offered by my wife Iris together with David's wife Enid and thanks are also due to John G.S. Smith without whose assistance this volume would not be so interesting and complete.

Publisher's Note

Increasingly photographers from far and wide are making material available for future editions of this series of books and there are some exciting prints now held on file for eventual use. If you ever photographed a London bus or coach, be it a single print or a larger number, or even took colour slides, then please do get in touch with the author. Many unsolicited letters have been received regarding the contents of the series of books which confirm that they are appreciated world wide by the devotees of the London bus. The author tries to acknowledge all letters received and is grateful for all the constructive comments which have been made. A listing of all identifiable London vehicles shown in the books so far published is now available *but only direct from the author at Dunstable*. It may be had in either route number order or fleet number order at a cost of £4.50 each inclusive of post and packing.

Introduction

Post-war standardisation of the bus and coach fleet, which had commenced in 1947, was finally achieved during the year with the last deliveries being made of RTs and RTLs. The initial orders for these vehicles had been placed soon after World War II had ended at the time when the manufacturing industries were gearing themselves up again for peace time production. Despite adjustments to the order books being made over the years to account for fluctuations in requirements, the Executive still found itself in the faintly embarrassing position in 1954 of having to put brand new vehicles when delivered into store, in some cases for as long as four years. Motor car ownership was making an increasing impact on the use of public transport and added to this television had started to change people's leisure habits and these trends were due to snowball over subsequent years.

Although by the end of the year an almost completely post-war passenger service fleet was now owned – the 2RT2s being the exception – it was not totally standard. In the double-deck category the RLH class made an interesting diversion and there were still post-war STLs and STDs running, not to mention the single Guy Arab. On the single deck front the GS class complemented the RFs but there were still post-war Ts and TDs, many of which still had a reasonable life expectancy.

Perhaps the highlight of the new vehicles delivered during the year was the first Routemaster, RM1, which made an appearance at the Commercial Motor Show although it would be 1956 before it entered public service. 296 RTs were received of which 181 were bodied by Park Royal and the remainder by Weymann. The Park Royal vehicles included those bodies which had previously been mounted on the now withdrawn SRT class and so the actual output from the north-west London factory was less than might have been supposed. 163 RTLs were delivered, 132 being bodied by Park Royal and 31 from Weymann. Apart from the odd RTL1307, which had been specially arranged for overseas tour purposes, these 31 were the first of the Leyland class to carry bodies from the Addlestone factory. Of this batch, numbered RTL1601-1631, only the first entered service in 1954 and the remainder gathered dust until four years later. The only other new vehicles were the balance of the ECW bodied GS class, which totalled 18.

Withdrawn vehicles totalled 509. This was made up of another 205 STLs, 67 STDs, 1 RT, 118 SRTs, 25 Ds, 85 Ts and 8 Cs. This meant the total eradication of three class letters from the stock list – SRT, D and C.

As far as route development was concerned 1954 was a quieter year than some of those which preceded it. At the beginning of the year a fairly big reorganisation of allocations took place when Nunhead garage closed resulting in some cases in former tram depots gaining work on routes where the tracks had never run. Services to new housing areas at places such as Debden, Borehamwood and Hayes North were developed. Other experiments like the 5 and 262 withered and perished after very short lives. Some long established patterns were changed, for example the 107 and 141 which intertwined at Borehamwood were replaced by a through 107 service and the Rochester Way and Eltham facility, linked since wartime days with Blackwall Tunnel, was linked instead to the route which had replaced the former 70 tram. There were new provisions such as the service to Downside Common on 215A and perhaps most noteworthy of all a service through the new tunnel at Heathrow (London Airport in 1954 terminology) to the "Central Enclosure" albeit only on summer Sundays. The other usual Summer Sunday extensions continued but a possible sign of things to come was the failure this year of 35A to go further into Epping Forest than the Royal Forest Hotel at Chingford.

In the Country Area apparent buoyancy must be considered against the fact of the developing New Towns which accounted for the upturn in traffic. The number of new routes meant that the long established sequence of 300 (north) and 400 (south) route numbers was exhausted and a new series of 800+ (north) and 851+ (south) was commenced. The Grays Green Line routes joined their Romford counterparts in East London by operating RTs from July onwards. Perhaps the most significant development was the introduction of three RFs fitted for one-man (no women at this stage!) operation. They first operated experimentally at Leatherhead on route 419 and then in August moved to Two Waters for a similar exercise on route 316.

Only one London Transport vehicle made a trip abroad during the year and this was RT4760 which was despatched to Maastricht in June at the request of the Board of Trade. It might have been necessary to describe where Maastricht was in 1954 but it is hardly so nowadays!

In many ways 1954 is a depressing year in London Transport history, both from the professional transport operator's point of view and from the enthusiast's. The former saw the downward spiral gaining momentum in relation to the number of passengers carried and vehicles owned while the latter had lost the variety and fascination of a multiplicity of types of vehicles to be seen on the streets of London.

The 26th May finds RT3024 from Cricklewood garage on route 226 and RT3348 from Rye Lane garage on route 12 at the Willesden Junction Hotel terminus in Harlesden. A typical builders' hand cart is parked near the kerbside while bits and pieces of his trade lie about, something that would not please today's Health and Safety Inspectors. (J.H. Aston)

Evidence of pre-war tram lines still show at the Wood Green end of Lordship Lane as crew operated RF424 from West Green garage takes passengers on board for the rest of its journey through the White Hart Lane Estate to Northumberland Park Station. Fourteen years later the 233 route would become W3 in which form it still exists to this day. The bus carries a "to and from" exhibition plate which no doubt refers to an event at Alexandra Palace, the high spot of a ride on this service. (Roy Marshall)

Weymann bodied T764 operating route 223 is pictured in the bus terminus at Uxbridge Underground station on the 4th July. From October 1934 up to the early war years all the lower 200 series route numbers were single deck operated but this demarcation was gradually eroded. Route 223 by this time was part double deck operated while 204, on which RT1903 behind is working, had been double deck from its introduction in 1951. (J.H. Aston)

RTLs replaced RTs at Dalston garage for route 47 earlier in the year although Bromley kept their RT allocation as witnessed by RT572, just included in the picture taken at Shoreditch Church on 13th July. RTL401, in true London Transport fashion, advertises the fact that some sort of problem has befallen it with a seat squab propped up against the platform rail. (J.H. Aston)

Route 408 stretched from Guildford in the south west extremity of the London Transport Country Area over to Warlingham, halfway across the southern operating sphere. Here, on the 5th June at Croydon, well laden RT2247 from Chelsham garage nears the end of its long haul. (J.H. Aston)

One of Holloway garage's small allocation on route 172, RT4160, is ready for its journey from Archway to Forest Hill at the allotted time of departure. This was the former Kingsway Subway tram service 35 and it would be another year before the 171 and 172 swopped their southern destinations. The advertisements would not look out of place in today's traffic, both products still being well known to shoppers. (J. Gascoine collection)

RT2398 lays over at Hendon Central Underground station on route 143 before returning to Highgate, Archway Station on the 15th July. This background has seen little change over the following years although the roundabout which enabled the stand to be placed here has long since disappeared. The premises "To Let" became a cafe frequented for some time by one of the compilers of these captions and although a runaway lorry did its best to demolish the station portico, it has now been duly restored. (J.H. Aston)

STD55 on the stand at the Red Lion in Pinner on the 23rd January. Car usage was already on the increase in this affluent area of North West London, as can be seen from the number parked up the road in front of the shops. The dolly stop for the terminal stand of route 220 from Uxbridge will not be needed this time next year. In December route 220 was cut back to Ruislip except for peak hours and weekends when it was extended to Northwood. (J.C. Gillham)

The experimental block inside Chiswick Works provides the resting place for PHW918, the Bristol LS6G, before its return to Bristol Tramways and Carriage Co. Ltd. The ECW bodywork appeared not to be quite so tidy around the window area when compared to the Metro Cammell bodied RF just visible in the picture but both are considered classics in their own right with many preserved examples still around. (J.C. Gillham)

An interesting view on the 23rd January of the rear of STD37 as passengers board at the Red Lion, Pinner on route 183 to "Golders Green L.T. Station". One wonders what other station at Golders Green the blind compiler imagined existed! Only STD1-100 and RT1 were ever adorned with the smaller variety of offside platform window and other than this small variation the Leyland bodywork on this batch of 100 vehicles, whilst distinctive to the expert, were a fair copy of new STLs of the same period of manufacture. (J.C. Gillham)

Park Royal bodied RT4278 is seen in Sutton on 6th April having been garaged at A since new in June of the previous year. Route 80 has a long history, having first commenced operation through Sutton for two weeks in 1916 before being axed in wartime economies, returning in 1919. At that time it came all the way from Charing Cross. (M.R.M. New)

Plumstead garage once had an allocation of single deckers for the 99 route and in later years they would return for that route but in 1954 their only experience with single deck operation was extremely brief. On 30th June new route 256 was introduced between Woolwich and Shooters Hill via Eglinton Hill and it was operated by one TD. TD71 was the usual vehicle and it stands here in General Gordon Place at Woolwich. The success was such that on 4th August the TD was replaced by an RTL and then on 4th January 1955 the route was absorbed into a variant of 89 numbered 89A. (G.A. Rixon)

The last red RT to be built by Weymann was RT4760 although the bus was originally intended to be painted green, being one of the last batch, numbered RT4722 to RT4794, delivered to the Executive. Owing to the then Board of Trade wanting to show the flag at a trade fair in Maastricht, Holland, a red London bus was deemed a necessity and the vehicle therefore attained the distinction of being the highest numbered red liveried Addlestone built product. The bus is pictured with a background of typical post-war built houses and very tidy gardens in the Dutch town whose name was hardly known until a certain recent Treaty wrote it firmly into the history books of the future. One of the British crew stands in military stance while a local transport company employee adopts a more casual approach. This tour to Holland was the only overseas trip made by a London Transport owned vehicle during the year. (Anglo-Iranian Oil Company)

This frontal view of RT44 as it makes its way past Euston station bound for Roehampton reminds one that few visual changes were made between the so called "pre-war" 2RT2 and the early post-war 3RT3. The slope down to the driver's cab windows and the destination box moved from above to below the intermediate box being the more obvious differences. The lighting on elegant standards and primitive but solid keep left bollards have long since gone but an open area in front of the station still remains as does the route, albeit only reaching Marble Arch. (G. Morant)

Nearing the end of its revenue earning career with London Transport, STL670, together with the taxi, appears to be doing little business. Despite the full blinds fitted, only an "end to end" blind is displayed in the destination box and the bus is presumably going home to its Dunton Green base.

RT10 carries Kingston garage plates while operating the Morden Station to Epsom Race Course special service and is seen here on the Downs taking passengers on board who are dressed against what must have been one of those colder race meetings. The age of the vehicles employed on this special service shows a considerable improvement over earlier years.

The dolly type bus stop announces "Sunday Bus Excursions" and a couple of passengers have taken advantage of RT3005 while it waits for more custom at Uxbridge for the Circular Tour of London, Excursion No. 6. Over to the left, camera at the ready, is possibly one of the intrepid photographers of the London bus. Does anybody recognise themselves and admit to being at Uxbridge on the 4th July?
(J.H. Aston)

The epitomised blind for route 489 carries no indication of the route taken on its short working to Longfield. Probably however all the passengers were regulars and "489" was sufficient. GS49 was operated by Northfleet garage for many years and does not carry a running number as it stands in Gravesend. (R.G. Bristow)

Swanley garage housed a representative selection of the then current Country Area vehicles when this photograph was taken. Beside RF264 on its way to Wrotham, which has stopped for a crew change, other stable mates stand in the garage. GS20, dressed for route 479, is the newest arrival and stands next to RT3882 which has its blinds set for route 401. The garage, usually referred to as Swanley Junction from its SJ code, is a typical piece of East Surrey Traction Company architecture although the building to the left is a London Transport style addition. (Lens of Sutton)

A passenger attempts to board RF590 as it sets out from Windsor to take up a short working on route 458 at Slough up to Iver. An interesting feature of all RFs was the clever incorporation of the London Transport hinged badge above the number plate which hid the filler cap and connection to the cooling system.

(J. Fozard)

This particular GS, number 41, appears to have escaped the preservation scene although someone may know different. Pictured in company with an RT ready for the long haul to Chelsham and a Green Line RF, the little Guy waits to run a journey to a destination almost within walking distance from Dorking Bus Station where it was photographed during September. (P. Gulland)

When the Grays Green Line routes were converted to operation with RTs on the 7th July the 723A was cut back to Grays and the section via Dock Road to Tilbury Ferry was replaced by a new 723B which followed the main 723 route between Aldgate and Grays thereby providing a more direct run through to the Ferry. Five days into service after its period of store at Loughton garage, RT4493 carrying a body previously mounted on SRT73 waits departure from London (Aldgate). (J.H. Aston)

RF700, one of the experimental one man operated RFs, stops in Epsom while working route 419. There is a "Pay As You Enter" sign on the nearside windscreen but it is hardly noticeable. This problem was one of a number of faults which showed up with the vehicles in service and in later years this sticker was replaced by an orange coloured lettered plastic board placed beneath the windscreen. (P. Gomm collection)

RT3877 about to pull away from a solidly constructed wooden bus shelter which apes the style of the standard LPTB metal structures of the pre-war years. The 403 route would in later years lose its considerable and very pleasant southern leg south of Chelsham down to Tonbridge and become a suburban operation which eventually turned red. (J. Gascoine collection)

A small number of the 15T13 type were transferred to Crawley garage during their career with London Transport. T784 is seen at The Plough, Dormansland, on the long route 434 from Horsham to Edenbridge via Troy Town. One wonders if any of the ladies on the bus are called Helen and will alight at this quaintly named hamlet on the western outskirts of Edenbridge! (A.B. Cross)

Photographed on the 15th May just after overhaul, Chalk Farm's RTL531 has as its backdrop St. James' Palace while turning into St. James' Street from Pall Mall. Since the bus is on Route 24 a fairly drastic diversion must have been in operation, probably occasioned by a State Visit. Route 24 had just converted from SRT operation and this was one of the replacing vehicles. (J.H. Price)

While working from Upton Park garage on route 101 to North Woolwich (Free Ferry) through the Royal Albert and King George V Dock area, STL1637 waits with other traffic while a big ship passes through. This particular route was destined to become the last one in the Central Area to operate the pre-war variety of this once numerous class. The crew take the opportunity to have a chat and the conductor jingles his loose change in his leather money bag while waiting. This bus, always a 4/9STL14, finished service with London Transport in June carrying body number 17039, which first appeared in service in January 1937 gracing the chassis of STL1744. (W. Legg)

Newspaper spread over the steering wheel, the driver of Potters Bar's RT1486 prepares to "higher up" his bus (as the LGOC used to call it) as it waits on the 134 stand at Victoria Station. The conductor is doubtless with the group of his or her colleagues by the battery of time clocks waiting for the appropriate time to clock out. (Lens of Sutton)

A bright sunny November finds RTL74 half in the shadows at Mitcham prior to the commencement of a journey to Acton Green on route 88. Riverside was the third garage to which this bus was allocated and it would remain there until moved out to Camberwell after its second overhaul in July 1957. (W. Legg)

Richard Costain Ltd. acquired this 9STL5, formerly STL730, during February from the Leeds dealer and, suitably identified, the vehicle makes quite a presentable means of transport for moving their employees around to the various construction sites. The little van parked behind almost looks as if it is a "Dinky" model placed to complete the picture.

New RTLs started to replace the SRTs used on route 24 from the 12th March. In gloomy conditions SRT133 is seen operating from Chalk Farm garage on this route long associated with the type. This was one of the later SRTs and carries the registration number of STL2103 whose chassis formed the basis of the hybrid vehicle. The Park Royal body would later be used in the construction of RT4527. (J. Gascoine)

Route 177 began life as a tram replacement route in 1952 operating between Abbey Wood and Victoria Embankment. Abbey Wood's RTL641, still to receive its first overhaul, looks superb in the livery in which it entered service back in 1950 as it heads towards town through Greenwich. (R.F. Mack)

On the 15th July many of the withdrawn members of the pre-war STD class stand in the Edgware garage yard together with home based RT1632 and STD118 which surprisingly carries an EW garage plate. PSV Circle records show this bus as allocated to Edgware for one month at this time but the purpose is an unsolved mystery. Note the differences in keeping out the elements afforded to the driver of the three types of vehicle shown here. No driver's door is fitted to STDs 90 and 97, while a hinged version is provided on the later STD with the familiar sliding unit on the RT. (J.H. Aston)

The different position of the offside route number plate on Saunders bodied RTs is well illustrated in this picture taken on the 27th August at Crystal Palace. Route 186 was a partial tram replacement route in 1952 covering the eastern end of Tram 72 from Woolwich to Lewisham and then replacing bus route 94 up to Crystal Palace. RT1182 is working the Catford garage allocation which was to disappear in the winter programme on 6th October. (J.H. Aston)

RF256, having just deposited the last of its passengers in Windsor High Street after its journey from Sevenoaks on route 705, will now run up to Windsor garage for a welcome layover. (J. Fozard)

RTL176 operating from Sidcup garage on route 161 stands at Parsons Hill, Woolwich with a trolleybus on one of the Bexleyheath routes just visible through the trees. A side blind is fitted as a makeshift resulting in two route numbers. Presumably a new supply of blinds is awaited since the temporary side blind is also an old one omitting the section of route between Woolwich and Eltham. (A.B. Cross)

Three London Ds with their original Brush or Duple built bodies await service in the Short Strand depot of Belfast Corporation. From left to right D64, 62 and 87 are seen in their new operator's livery and carrying fleet numbers 469, 467 and 474 before their appearance changed completely when new Harkness bodywork was fitted in 1955. (R. Ludgate)

Entering service during May from Walworth garage, RTL1508 reflects the sun from its prestige condition while driver and conductor pause for discussion. Route 36A was one of a number affected by the closure of Nunhead garage, the route, although unrelated to that garage, lost its Peckham allocation of 16RTs and that from Walworth was increased by a similar number. (W. Legg)

Having spent a while as a special bus at Riverside garage, T706 is now returned to passenger service from Grays garage. For two months during the summer a ride on this vehicle, first put into service in 1938, was a possibility in this Thames-side Essex town before, in August, the more affluent Windsor, much further up river, became its operational base. Here it stands by Rainham Church working the short 375 route down to Rainham Ferry, although the blind is set for an even shorter shuttle between the level crossing at the railway station and the Ferry. Although this route disappeared off the Country Area Bus Map after the 1948 edition it continued operating at certain times for a further ten years. (Lens of Sutton)

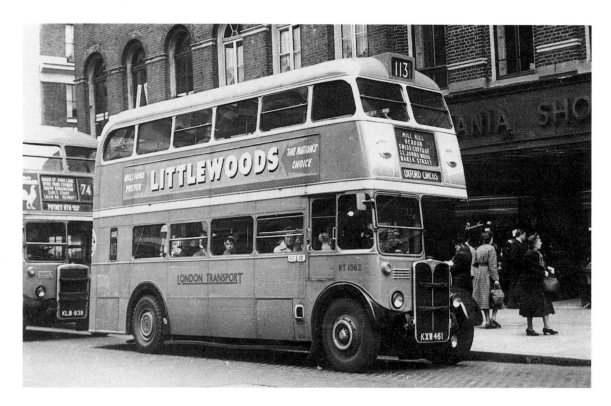

The unmistakable engine note of a Leyland STD bus on route 113 is now a thing of the past. The new order had taken over in the form of the AEC and RT1362 from Hendon garage is seen in Baker Street with RTW209 working route 74 from Putney Bridge garage behind. It looks as though steps have been taken to remove the word "ONLY" from the Putney Heath, Green Man destination of the RTW. (G. Morant)

RF300 carrying registration number MLL937 stands at the Wallington terminus of route 234A. Two years on, when additional buses were converted to coach use, the bus would exchange its fleet number with RF519 in the tidy-minded exercise to keep coaches and buses numerically in the same batch. (Roy Marshall)

The date is the 27th August and the location Crystal Palace with RT4297 operating from Victoria garage on route 137. This RT had first seen service from Willesden garage before being transferred to its present home in February of this year. Route 137 had its origins in the well known Birch/City independent route 536 being re-routed in South London to Clapham Common in 1937 and then breaking new ground through Kings Avenue and Leigham Court Road when it was extended to Crystal Palace the following year. (J.H. Aston)

The 93 route made its usual summer extension through to Dorking at Easter and on high summer Sundays during the year. RT31 is about to enter – or is it backing out of? – Dorking garage on Good Friday the 16th April. Holiday and Sunday outings by ordinary bus service were still popular in 1954 although the privately owned car was beginning to make inroads. (A.B. Cross)

The Chelverton Road, Putney garage training vehicle for just over six months from August was green liveried STL975. This bus entered service in February 1935, being one of a batch of 89 front entrance LPTB 48 seat vehicles built for the Country Area. In order to form a float of this type of body for overhaul purposes, four of these STL6 bodies were removed from their chassis and replaced by 56 seat rear entrance examples in August 1939. This bus was one of the four and received this STL14/1 body which remained married with the chassis throughout the rest of its existence with London Transport.

RT4058 spent its early days with London Transport in store at Edgware garage before entering service from Turnham Green and eventually finding itself in service on route 265, a variation of the 65 route. Here, outside the imposing Acton Town Station which had been rebuilt in 1932, it makes its way to the Coach and Horses at Kew Green on a short working at the northern end of the route. During 1954 the off peak Monday to Friday service on route 265 was split into two unconnected sections form East Acton to Kew Green and Kingston to Chessington.
(J. Gascoine collection)

Two Alperton RTs – 2773 and 539 – working the Edgware to Wembley weekday section of Route 18, provide a good illustration of the development of blind styles. The further bus has the original style, while RT2773 nearest the camera shows the later style of one place name per line. In fact this is unusual in being only four lines, that style being a later development, but if you were restricting the design to using place names only then there were only four available for this blind. (J.H. Aston)

RTL115 makes its way on a short working, presumably through late running, to Gants Hill Station. Seven Kings garage was home for the vehicle which had previously been garaged at Riverside until it was overhauled and transferred during the year under review. (A.B. Cross)

The Tilling ST bodied AEC Regent Mark III chassis number 0961079 was for many years used as a training vehicle for engineering staff and was first shown in the 1949 book of this series. This photograph gives a clear view of the platform area and open staircase arrangement. Soon after this photograph was taken outside the main office block in Chiswick Works the body was scrapped and the chassis was fitted with a Weymann body to become RT4761 1954. (J.C. Gillham)

Time marches on, as the saying goes, and of a bygone age are the RF and RT together with the open expanse of parking area in front of Dorking Bus Station. RF182, in the condition in which it was delivered, waits to take up duties as DS35 along the roads followed by Route 713 to Dunstable, some 70 plus miles to the north. This particular Green Line link between these two distant towns was finally withdrawn on the last day of May 1975. (P. Gomm collection)

Photographed in tranquil surroundings with the village church tower clock indicating five to five, former STL1697 seems to have found peace and quiet at long last after its hurly burly days in London. Even the blind says "Relief"! The bus was operated by Premier Travel Ltd. of Cambridge as their number 89 for around six years before it was finally put to rest for good. (Lens of Sutton)

Green liveried RT1418, in use as a Green Line relief and operating between London and Windsor, waits beside the rudimentary passenger shelters on Eccleston Bridge before returning to its home town and garage. It would appear to have been a nice warm day, judging by the number of open windows in evidence on the bus. (J. Gascoine collection)

Garston garaged RT3816 about to pull away from the bus stop in Rectory Road, Rickmansworth en route for Luton on route 321A. This variation of the trunk 321 route had been introduced on 7th October of the previous year by extending Luton – Rickmansworth short journeys up to Berry Lane Estate. (R.H.G. Simpson)

Craven bodied RT1500 waits immediately outside the portals of Morden Underground station. The building and the Underground extension was opened in 1926 and the terminus was first used by a new system of bus routes introduced at the time and radiating from the forecourt. The 164 has undergone considerable changes over the years but originally it was one of those routes running then to Burgh Heath. Local Authorities tried to bring pressure to bear to obtain an extension of the tube to Epsom in the nineteen thirties but this was rejected since the capacity from Morden northwards was already overstretched. (A.B. Cross)

These two views of STL1856 clearly show the differing interior finish of an STL11 body, better known as the "Tunnel" variety. Forty of these specially designed bodies were manufactured by the LPTB for fitting on to STL chassis and in turn they replaced NS type vehicles on the two routes through the Blackwall and Rotherhithe Tunnels. On the upper deck the staircase enters at right angles to the gangway having completed a "U" shaped route from the platform area. The two single seats allow room for this. The arched roof is in evidence resulting in reduced headroom for passengers when rising from the window seats. The lower saloon picture shows more detail differences, the offside longitudinal seat has been reduced from the usual 3 to 2 passengers because of the modified staircase. This particular STL first entered service in March 1937 being withdrawn in January of this year to be disposed of to W. North, the dealer, who found a buyer in the form of the contractors, Lovatt, who then operated the vehicle for a number of years. (J.C. Gillham)

As part of the knock-on effect of the closure of Nunhead garage on 6th January, Route 179, which was then running from Farringdon Street to Grove Park, was re-allocated from Rye Lane to New Cross. In a sense this was a homecoming since New Cross tram depot had always operated the 74 tram route which it had replaced in 1952. On the 9th January RT1430 picks up passengers outside stores involved in January sales including the gentleman's outfitters, Meakers, of blessed memory! (A.B. Cross)

Space is getting more restricted at the Belmont Station terminus for route 213 as evidenced in this view of RF298 squeezed between the kerb and parked cars. The Central Area batch of this class was coded 2RF2 and the vehicles had seats for 41 passengers, no platform doors and were the only variety to be fitted with a route number plate above the doorway, although often, as in this case, it was not used. (A.B. Cross)

Chelsham garaged RT2508 pauses at Warlingham Green on its short but hilly journey on Route 453 to Caterham on the Hill while behind RT3141, operated by Leatherhead since its overhaul in February, lays over on the much more lengthy route 470 via Croydon, Epsom and Leatherhead to Dorking. The picture was taken on the 5th June. (J.H. Aston)

Chalk Farm garage had only a few months to operate SRT152 which had been transferred there in the autumn of the previous year before route 24, normally associated with this type of bus, would be converted to RTL operation during April. The Park Royal body depicted here later reappeared as Country Area RT4541 allocated to Epping garage. (A.B. Cross)

Route 81B, operated by Hounslow garage, first ran as a Saturday and Sunday only route for the 1954 Summer season commencing on 22nd May. It used the newly constructed road tunnel beneath the runways at London Airport to reach what was called "The Central Enclosure". Aircraft buffs will be interested in the planes in the background while security minded readers may well disbelieve the scene. A good number of passengers are boarding RT858 before it makes its way back to Hounslow. It would seem that this bus has not been equipped with a new 'via blind' and misleadingly shows a main 81 route display. (D.A. Jones)

Lightly loaded RT3814 is seen as it makes its way to Beaconsfield on route 305, which in 1954 only ran from Gerrards Cross. Only three lines of via points were needed for this horseshoe shaped operation. The blind over the platform is a front blind lacking a route number. When new this particular vehicle, together with others from the small Weymann bodied batch painted green and numbered RT3807 to 3816, was operated from the Central Area at Southall.

(J. Gascoine collection)

RT4352 operating from Merton garage with RTL1537, one of Battersea's contingent for the same 49 route, waits at Shepherds Bush Green. Note the unrepaired tree damage to the front nearside of the leading bus, much less common then than nowadays and note also the continued use of Brylcreem by smart young men of the day.

(Roy Marshall)

RF24 parked in the Putney Bridge garage yard where in views shown in earlier years of this series of books LTs, STs and STLs once stood. The date is 15th August and although the private hire coach is now three years old it still looks immaculate enhanced by the attractive colour scheme adopted for these 27½ feet long vehicles. (J.H. Aston)

Once T543 and now Split Transport number 30, this 10T10 is seen at Trogir on 29th April while operating service number 1 (Split to Trogir). Still in its London red livery which it gained in January 1952 and carrying its former British registration number, it has gained an offside folding door to cope with the rule of the road in Yugoslavia. The bus had been disposed of to W. North in August 1953 together with a large number of similar vehicles. (D.W.K. Jones)

The last route to use the pre-war version of the STD class was the 183 which ran from Golders Green Station to Northwood Station and had been home to these fine vehicles ever since their introduction in 1937. In this crowded view taken at Golders Green one of the replacement RTs has already filtered into use on the route and waits in front of STD75.

These two interior views of D217 were taken on the 15th January before the bus left for W. North, the dealers, later in the month. It was on the 8th when the final members of this class, which once totalled 281, were withdrawn from service in London. This is one of the relaxed utility specification vehicles operated by Sutton garage and classified 3/1D4. The body included six opening windows on each side set in pans, standard post-war moquette on tubular steel seat frames and lighter colour from midway up the window height. (J.C. Gillham)

Works services in the Country Area have always posed problems for crews in displaying correct blinds and those in Gravesend to Rosherville down by the Thames below Overcliffe were no exception. The 495A from Christianfields Estate looks very tidy although the canopy blind still shows 480 as does the 488A behind which has come from Kings Farm Estate. The two buses, RT2252 and 3680, were obviously derived from the allocation of the trunk Erith – Denton service. (Lens of Sutton)

By 1954 the former Festival of Britain routes to Battersea Park from South Kensington and Sloane Square were renumbered 45A and 137A respectively and made their first appearance of the year on Good Friday. RT1937 operating from Norwood garage waits within Battersea Park on route 137A. This view typifies Londoners enjoying the pleasures of London's open spaces on a fine day in Spring. (J. Gascoine collection)

The London fleet replacement which commenced in 1947 was finally completed during the year. Many operators throughout the British Isles and in some foreign lands took advantage of the varied fleet of well maintained vehicles released by London Transport. The chassis of this NCME lowbridge bodied vehicle registered FSD454 once belonged to G130. Having been purchased by Western SMT in 1953 it was subsequently stripped down and rebuilt, given new chassis number RB/51/1 before being transformed into this 'tin fronted' unrecognisable ex-London bus. It is seen here at the operator's Johnstone garage having just been delivered from the coach builders in June. (Ian Maclean)

Beaconsfield is one of those country area towns, thankfully unchanged and not spoilt too much by the developers. The M40 motorway having taken much of the traffic off the A40 which passes through this delightful 'olde world' town ensures that it stays in its time warp. GS52 stands in front of the inconspicuous Lloyds Bank which looks as if its role should be that of the vicarage to the Parish Church of St. Mary and All Saints, which can be visited through the gate behind the bus. (R.H.G. Simpson)

The date is 21st February and RT1283 is pictured at London Bridge Station on this Sunday duty of route 10. Restricted blinds were still to be seen but increasingly they were becoming fewer and fewer. Probably the opportunity to fit full blinds to this Saunders bodied RT had to wait until May when it received its first overhaul. (A.B. Cross)

Rows of new green liveried RTs are stored within Loughton garage sitting on their brake drums having had their wheels and tyres removed. RT4753 and RT4788 can be identified from the large number of buses collecting dust. The entire last batch of Weymann built green liveried RTs ignominiously found themselves stored in this way, either at the above mentioned garage or at Garston and in some cases it would be five years before they would enter service. (A.B. Cross)

Photographed on the 25th May at Aldgate, SRT124 carries the older type of blinds associated with route 42 in the days of restricted apertures. (J.H. Aston)

One of the last 60 seat LGOC STL1 type bodies that could be seen on the streets of London was body 13556, first carried by STL170. By 1941 the body was one of a number in the float system held at Chiswick works and it was duly mounted on to a new chassis delivered in the first month of 1942, emerging from the works in February of that year as STL2679. This combination of newer chassis and 1933 built body continued in London Transport ownership till October 1954. The bus is seen here at the rebuilt Hounslow bus garage being used as a staff bus and carrying trade plate 081GF. Eventually the body would be scrapped and the chassis used to form the basis of service vehicle 1009J. (M. Rooum)

A fine study of ex-G356 as it makes its way through Perth to the Scott Street terminus of W. Alexander & Sons' route 11A. The matured stone built buildings, typical of this city, contrast sharply with the austere lines of the Guy Arab bus, now carrying fleet number R0722 and a Perth garage plate.

STL1613, a 3/9STL12, was by 1954 owned by R.W. Hooks of Great Oakley, Essex, who never put the bus to good use. Subsequently in 1955 it was noted as a showman's vehicle. It would seem from this picture that local children considered the vehicle to be a play bus some years before the concept of such vehicles was thought of. (Roy Marshall)

Eccleston Bridge and RF245 working from Dunton Green continues its journey through to Windsor. In the background is a type of London taxi, less numerous than the Austin variety but still common in its day and produced by the Nuffield Corporation. The model was probably a casualty of the Austin-Morris merger which took place in the early fifties. (M. Banks)

At Edgware, with members of the withdrawn 1STD1 type of bus in the background, RTW3 attracts a number of passengers as it waits to take up service on route 18 to Wembley, Empire Pool. This is a location that is totally unrecognisable today with a new Bus Station and shopping complex. (A.B. Cross)

RTW197 with RT2550 parked behind and RTL897 to its left wait at an overcrowded Camden Gardens stand before departing for their southern destinations. The scene is even more depressed with the heavily pruned skeletons of the trees awaiting their summer plumage which should greatly improve the image of this terminus for routes 3, 39 and 53. (W. Legg)

The small scale experiment to make use of the traffic indicator arms is evidenced here by the black oblong aperture and arm in place underneath running plates D13 carried by RTL489. Quite obviously they were still not considered reliable or functional and work on their replacement would commence, culminating in experimental trafficators being fitted to a number of buses in 1956 with full scale fitment to the fleet from 1959 onwards. The date is the 13th July and the location the Liverpool Street terminus of route 9 with Mortlake garage's RT1389 as the following bus on the route. (J.H. Aston)

These interior views of Brush bodied D95 show the original leather seating provided on the thirty five buses delivered in the period June 1945 through to October 1945. The coverings were never replaced and were still fitted when these pictures were taken on the 20th January. Earlier examples of D class buses from this source had either been fitted with wooden slatted seats, which were replaced some years later, or with moquette finished seating. Five opening windows on each side had been fitted from new but this particular bus was the last from this manufacturer to have the more angular dome as evidenced in the view looking rearwards on the upper deck. For four years after its sale by London Transport, T.D. Alexander, operating as Greyhound Coaches of Sheffield, used the bus as their number 27 before disposing of it to a contractor in the Birmingham area in 1959. (J.C. Gillham)

Where once the Daimler D class reigned supreme an RT from the many thousands now on the road will be a familiar sight for many years to come at Morden Station. On the 17th April RT232, operating from Sutton garage, pauses on its way to Reynolds Close at Hackbridge. (A.B. Cross)

Route 203 was converted to RT operation in 1954 but STL571 was still giving yeoman service during the Spring. Several passengers have alighted and the conductor rings the bus off to continue its journey to Hatton Cross. So good was the condition of the bus that it eventually found its way to the Canary Islands where no doubt it enjoyed even more sunshine.

The date is the 27th February and RF379 picks up passengers at Sutton on its journey to Kingston Bus Station. The bus was delivered new to Norbiton garage being one of a number put into service during the latter part of 1952 and the early months of 1953 which displaced the single deck LT class that once operated this route. (A.B. Cross)

Negotiating Oxford Circus on route 23 to Barking garage, RTL327 is the centrepiece of an interesting period street scene. Firstly, there is the policeman on point duty supplementing the traffic lights. Then, a large Humber car of 1948 or later manufacture follows the bus while the rear end of a new Austin taxi can just be seen travelling in the opposite direction. (Roy Marshall)

The 4th July looks as if it could have turned out to be a rather nice day. RF598 stands at Uxbridge, roughly where the garage entrance is now, with doors open inviting passengers to board and sit down while waiting to commence their journey. In the background an RT waits for patrons fancying a trip round Central London by way of Excursion Number 6. (J.H. Aston)

The conductor of West Green's RTL375 confers with his driver after the bus has arrived at the setting down stop for the Alexandra Park (Victoria Hotel) terminus of route 144A. The blind has already been re-set for the return short working to the Halfway House at Enfield which was the route's ultimate terminus prior to May 1953. Since the 144A and 144B routes now bore little affinity with 144 they were renumbered 217 and 231 respectively on the 19th May. (M. Rooum)

GS32 was one of six vehicles of the class delivered in 1953 to replace older C class at Dunton Green and is seen here at Orpington Station at the terminal stop which has changed little over the years. Preservationist John Clarke, a member of the RF/RT Register is now the proud owner of this vehicle which is steadily being returned to its former glory. (M. Rooum)

The Odeon Astoria cinema at Brixton advertising its newest attraction for "Monday Next", 'The Kidnappers', provides a backcloth for RTL408 as it operates from Clapham garage on route 45. The boards with their customary six "stills" from the picture were a feature of every cinema at the time although how effective they were in attracting custom is open to debate. However regular cinema going was so prevalent that it probably didn't matter what you put up outside. (W. Legg)

One of the small number of 15T13s, which were transferred to Crawley garage in the summer of 1953, is seen here at The George in Crawley's old town centre. Route 426 was a circular service from Crawley through Horley which originated as East Surrey route 26 and by 1954 had a separate section running between Ifield and Three Bridges on which T787 is operating. On 10th August this section, which ran via Gales Drive, was renumbered 426A.

RTL642, carrying full blinds in a livery which had been replaced by the single cream band between decks version in 1950, makes a welcome visual impact as it operates on route 41 to Tottenham Hale in place of one of the allocated RTWs. Having been delivered to the Executive in February 1950 the bus still had a few more months before gaining its first overhaul in September. There is no way that the modern DIY stores can compensate for the loss of shops like that of Mr. Loft seen by this bus stop in West Green Road. The right nut and bolt or tool would always be found for you and helpful advice proffered on whatever was the task in hand. Unfortunately the picture cannot recapture that wonderful smell of such establishments. (P.J. Marshall)

Both vehicles, if anything is to be construed from their registration plates, are recent acquisitions to the transport scene at Sibenik in Yugoslavia. The interesting bus with regard to this series of books is of course T490, now registered H6152. This was one of the large batch mentioned in the caption to T543 seen elsewhere in the book. This one, however, retains its two tone Green Line colours. (D.W.K. Jones)

As part of the Omnibus Society Silver Jubilee celebrations a parade of veteran buses was arranged to run from the Commercial Motor Show at Earls Court to Piccadilly Circus on Saturday 25th September. Here heavily laden B340 dating from 1911 and one of the world's first major standardised motor bus fleet, negotiates Piccadilly. The driver of the 2RT2 on Route 14 would seem to be in conversation with the gentleman precariously riding the platform step. (J.C. Gillham)

These two interior views of seven year old T766 show the bus as a 33 seater, the double transverse seats on each wheel arch having been replaced by single longitudinals in January 1950. The date is 13th April, a few months before the seating would be further reduced by one seat when the front offside double seat was replaced by a single seat to give the conductor a less trampled on standing position. The bodybuilder's initials are proudly embellished on the clutch housing cover below the fare board for route 211, which indicates its allocation to Southall garage. The decor was brown with the top strip of beading above the windows painted green and standard London Transport moquette to an otherwise provincial style body. (J.C. Gillham)

Always garaged at Watford High Street for its comparatively short life with London Transport, RT1406 operating route 306 waits on the stand at New Barnet Station. This was a convenient turning point for many years for Country Bus routes from the north but alas not even the present day successors to the handsome Lincoln green vehicles get anywhere near nowadays. (M. Rooum)

STL1742 in its last months of operation is seen in Romford while working to Harold Hill, Dagnam Park Drive, on route 66A. This was one of the routes having experimental route blinds with large type and fewer places named and the effect is quite pleasing on this pre-war vehicle.
(J. Gascoine Collection)

Once B20 and now 2109 in the Lincolnshire Road Car Company's fleet, this vehicle, together with eight others of the type, saw many year's service with their new operator. They always carried their original bodies but, as can be seen here, they were altered over the years. The renewed front upper deck windows contrast with all the other square cornered windows fitted. (J. Gascoine Collection)

The port of Dover played host in the 1950s to a very different form of road transport to the present day juggernauts that ply their way to the Continent. Standing beneath the cliffs two British exports, green STL491, together with an unidentifiable example, await their turn to make the short trip across the Channel. The advertisement on STL491 is possibly a little misleading at Dover.

This somewhat intriguing view was taken on 26th May at Willesden Junction and it suggests that "an event" of some description is taking place. The freshly painted barrier, well dressed lady and, further on, behatted gentleman together with assorted goods wagons including a spotless looking fish van leads one to this conclusion. RFW11, which has possibly brought a party to the event, reminds one of the coaching days of the 1950s. Hinged front opening passenger door, glass louvres to the windows, traffic arm indicators and glass cant windows are indicative of a bygone age. (J.H. Aston)

The date is the 25th April and RT34 occupies the familiar stand above the railway in Oxford Road at Putney. By this time several of the so-called "pre-war RTs" had received full blinds but regrettably the rear roof route number box, unique to these vehicles, was not brought back into use. Note however that, unlike the RT3 variety of body, the ultimate destination is above the intermediate point blind and was changed by the conductor. (W. Legg)

By the end of the month Q132 would be on its way to its eventual destruction but now waits sadly on the 20th January among the litter and rubble at Chiswick works. In the early spring all the remaining members of this class were despatched to a dealer in the north and none of this last batch appear to have escaped the breakers' torches. (J.C. Gillham)

The solid institutional buildings at Moorgate provide the background to Old Kent Road's RT1495 as it sets out on route 21 southwards to Sidcup Garage. (C. Carter)

A Bedford "S" type lorry together with a Morris Commercial van mingle with the London buses in this view taken at Oxford Circus. The centrepiece, Craven bodied RT1455, heads for "Holborn Stn Only" on route 7A, London Bridge being the ultimate destination of the route. The "To and From White City" slipboard on this bus is a little misleading since the 7A turned down Ducane Road at Wormwood Scrubs, leaving passengers to make their way across Western Avenue to get to the White City Stadium. RTL530 follows in the convoy while a route 60 bus turns into Regent Street. (R. Marshall)

Two interior photographs of an STL20 body, in this case STL2688. Built by Weymann soon after the cessation of World War II, they were of that company's standard provincial design and completely lacked any "London" features. Note the position of the interior nearside concertinered blind to cover the bulkhead window at night which almost looks like an afterthought. (J.C. Gillham)

1954 was reputed to have been a very wet summer but 15th August was by all accounts a beautiful day with the side windows of RTL1110 all in the open position and the driver having rolled up the sleeves of his summer weight coat. The location is the Green Man, Putney Heath and the bus, minus a running number, appears to be about to run in to the garage at Wandsworth at the end of the day. (J.H. Aston)

SRT159 operating on route 42 which stayed loyal on Mondays to Fridays to this class of bus until the last day of their operation at the end of July after which they were replaced by RTLs.
(J. Gascoine Collection)

RLH76, the last numbered of this small class of low height buses seen at Langley Avenue, North Cheam on the 22nd March. Merton garage required their complement of these attractive provincial style vehicles for route 127 which passed under the then low bridge at Worcester Park Station. The route was withdrawn in 1958 in the first stage of the Central area bus cuts following the disastrous strike of that year. Later on the road under the railway bridge at Worcester Park was lowered which allowed normal height vehicle operation in the area.
(J.G.S. Smith collection)

The GS class is very popular with preservationists forty years on and examples turn up all over the country at bus rallies. GS17 is one such bus and since 1990 has been under new ownership who are keen that it should be seen around its former haunts in north west Hertfordshire. In its early days however it was allocated to Leatherhead at which garage it is seen ready for duty on the local 481 service at Epsom. In the 1948 book of this series a CR vehicle can be seen working the route.

(G.A. Rixon)

Tottenham's RTW69 operates one of that garage's Sunday only duties on route 144 on the 21st February. It is standing at the York Road terminal in Ilford reached via Beal Road and Argyle Road. The 144 was one of the routes initially allocated the 8 feet wide Leylands but subsequently lost them to more central routes. Tottenham's involvement however returned some to the route for a while. (A.B. Cross)

Standardisation at Morden Station is portrayed by Sutton garage's RTs 2493, 1160 and 1500 where Daimlers once mingled. At least the Craven body on 1500 and the Saunders body on 1160 provide a little relief from the monotony after the variation of years gone by. (A.B. Cross)

TF25, photographed in April after its conversion to an open lorry for the delivery of milk churns and here seen well loaded at Wheatley Hill, County Durham. Most of the passenger area has been removed and only its unmistakable LPTB front quarter remains. It is not known what Mr. Dowson, the owner, thought of the vehicle but it was certainly unique. See the book for 1952 for a picture of the vehicle in service on route 391. (R. Hobbs/A.B. Cross)

The short lived and little used route 262 ran for the last time on the 2nd March. RT1201 was allocated to Sutton garage during January just prior to it receiving an overhaul, after which it was despatched to Hornchurch. Here in Cheam Village it stands empty as usual before a further wander down Sandy Lane on the short route to Cuddington. (P.J. Marshall)

STL1262 originally carried a Dodson 52 seat body from ex-Daimler DST5, which had been acquired with the Redline fleet taken over by LPTB in 1933. That body was damaged during the war and was removed in August 1944, a standard ST body replacing it. Late in 1946 the chassis was rebuilt and extended and fitted with a standard STL body. By the time the bus was disposed of in April 1954 it was carrying body number 17949, an STL12 variety. It is seen here at Chiswick Works on 3rd March in company with STL2397. The mixture of blinds is a little odd. Night route 286 obviously comes from a Peckham blind gained while carrying out training duties from that garage in 1953. The 86A is more of a mystery since there is no record of allocation to any of the various East London garages concerned with this route. (J.C. Gillham)

The stand at Wandsworth Plain in south west London provides the resting place for Craven bodied RT1513 operating from Middle Row garage on route 28 on this warm 15th August. This RT had gained an overhaul in December of the previous year having first been put to work from Cricklewood garage in February 1950. Subsequently sold to the Ayrshire Bus Owners (A1) in April 1956, the bus would be the last serviceable Craven bodied RT with that operator when finally withdrawn in September 1970. (J.H. Aston)

Nunhead garage closed on the night of 5th/6th January. Originally owned by the National Steam Car Company and built in 1912, the building still stands today; someone having the foresight to get it listed. Here RT4091 works the long standing Nunhead route 63 to Kings Cross about to be taken over by Peckham garage. Later in the year this route would be extended on 15th September from Honor Oak to Crystal Palace via Sydenham Hill in lieu of the Crystal Palace High Level rail service which finished three days later. This was the second London suburban branch railway closure of the year, the other being that to North London's equivalent of the Crystal Palace, the Alexandra Palace in May. (J. Gascoine Collection)

RTs at Chalk Farm garage were a short lived phenomenon in 1954, eight being received from Twickenham who in turn received some new green ones for a while. RT1716 is seen during its two months stay at the North London garage after which it returned to its home in the south west. It is seen at the Greenland Road stand at Camden Town on the incredibly stable 31 route which had worked here from Chelsea since 1916 and still does to this day. (P.J. Marshall)

Route 70A was withdrawn after 16th March and the peak hour service it provided between the Victoria Embankment and London Bridge was replaced in part by an extension of some 168s as route 168A. Unlike the 70A, which went over Blackfriars Bridge to Southwark Street as did its tramway predecessors, the 168A ran via Queen Victoria Street and Southwark Bridge. The route existed for exactly one year, last day of operation being 15th March 1955. Here Clapham garage's RTL883 is ready to run to London Bridge on this little photographed route. (N. Rayfield)

Waterloo Place at the bottom of Lower Regent Street was the unique terminal approved by the Police for the Ominbus Society's Silver Jubilee run from the Earls Court Commercial Motor Show on the 25th September. NS1995, one of four vehicles sent by London Transport had dropped behind due to overheating several times on the run. However, the driver attributed this to the slow speed of the procession saying that his "27 year young vehicle preferred a smarter pace". How many OS members will be able to recognise themselves in the selection of photographs taken on this historic occasion? (J.C. Gillham)

TD24 originally entered service from Muswell Hill garage in February 1947 and still resided there when this photograph was taken on the 15th July. Its departure from this garage to Kingston took place in January 1957. Operating as duty MH2 on the 251 route from Burnt Oak to Arnos Grove, it stands in Barnfield Road at the Burnt Oak terminus. (J. H. Aston)

RF325 is seen on the same day as TD24 on route 251 on the same Burnt Oak stand. This was an unusual working at such an early date, a scheduled partial RF allocation not appearing until 1955. This bus was one of Muswell Hill's original allocation for route 210. (J. H. Aston)

The Montague Arms at Roehampton provides the background to RT287 which worked from Middle Row garage from new until moved away to Sidcup in 1955. This is a short working on Route 72 which, in 1954, still ventured down the Kingston-by-Pass to Esher. Middle Row's involvement in 1954 was only on Summer Sundays when six buses were allocated to supplement the more usual Riverside vehicles. (J.H. Aston)

The three lightweight experimental single deckers loaned to the Executive in the period 1953 – 1954 were all moved from their Country Area duties to Central Area routes 208/A for a few months before being returned to their rightful owners in the Spring. Photographed here at Clapton Pond on a wintry looking day, Bristol PHW918 lays over before journeying to Bromley by Bow and now sports a London Transport fleetname in place of the previously carried Green Line.
(John Gascoine collection)

Standing at Clapham Common, while resting before commencing the long return journey to Chingford Hatch, Leyton garaged RT1441, a Craven built product operates duty T22. Parked further along the road Saunders bodied RT4219 waits to take up duties on route 137 while garaged at Victoria. (W.Legg)

By now STL222 was the lowest numbered of the class still to be seen on the roads of the Capital and leaves Aldenham works fully laden as a staff bus for its homeward bound journey to Southall. Its original registration number was AGX563 but now it runs under trade plates 294GC in a capacity for which these plates are no longer allowed. Having entered service in September 1933 as a Central Area bus it gained its green livery in June 1941 and is still in this livery. The bus was disposed of to Birds the dealers of Stratford upon Avon in the last month of the year under review. (Lens of Sutton)

Before the RF class had been put into service a single deck LT would have been the normal bus to have operated route 227 but sadly time marches on. Bromley garages's RF344 now stands under the leafless trees at Crystal Palace on the 20th February together with RTL628 on route 186 which is still awaiting its first overhaul. (J.H. Price)

The rubber pads set in the roadway to activate traffic lights are another feature which has almost disappeared from the streets of the capital to be replaced by sensors let into the road surface. The location is Clapham Common, the date is 23rd March and the bus RTL495 which was outshopped, having had its first overhaul, in the previous month. (W. Legg)

RF308 in its original condition as a Central Area bus and registered MLL945. It operates from Dalston garage on route 208 which has over the years played host to some interesting and innovative vehicles. This route with its many sharp corners, narrow roads, cobbled surfaces and heavy loadings was a test for any vehicle and the RF type responded well. (P.J. Marshall)

RT2007 operating from the ex-Tilling garage at Croydon waits at the West Croydon terminus of route 64 before working a short journey to Selsdon, Farley Road on a warm 5th June. The windscreen wiper has been moved out of the way which was often the case in prolonged fine weather spells. (J.H. Aston)

STL742 gained Country Area colours in January 1952 and operated in this new guise till being withdrawn in June 1954. Here in the Grays garage yard it stands next to RT1055 and the two vehicles make an interesting comparison. Note the spindle for a starting handle on the STL and the variation of layout on the blinds which was to yet again reverse itself in years to come. Having been in service from June 1935 the STL rather surprisingly still carries its original body, being number 15157, one of a batch of 200 similar STL5/1 LPTB built examples. (Lens of Sutton)

Just a small point I know but some of the class of GS vehicles appear to have been fitted with hand grips at the bottom of the front windscreen while others were not so fitted. GS71 has the handles and also carries a paper sticker in the upper right hand corner of the windscreen asking you to "please pay as you enter and tender exact fare". It is at Broxbourne on its way from Hoddesdon to Harlow on the 393 route. (A.B. Cross)

The small canopy box route number blind carried by RT1515 in its roof box spoils the look of this Craven bodied RT as it heads out through East London on Route 25 on 21st February. The word "ONLY" added to the Becontree Heath destination is pedantically correct since the route still had a peak hour extension to Hornchurch. The terminus at Becontree Heath however would be the old one at James Avenue, the new private lay by in Wood Lane, east of the Three Travellers public house, not being brought into use until 5th July. (A.B. Cross)

Route 79 operated between Perivale, Bideford Avenue and Colindale where this picture is taken. Guys were operated on this route, being replaced by older STLs among which STL2477, the "Meccano Set", was a regular performer for some time. The last STL left the route in March since when Alperton garage has used RTs and here Craven bodied RT1453 waits for its departure time. (J.H. Aston)

Where does a G become a D? The answer is Mombassa. Former G86 is seen operating for Kenya Bus Services under its new fleet number D54. Presumably the D meant diesel or double-deck or perhaps Guy in Swahili – who knows! Service in this warmer clime was relatively short lived since the bus was scrapped during 1957 after an accident. The vehicle's Park Royal built body appears basically unchanged except for some modification around the platform area and, one suspects, permanently open windows. Peek Frean biscuits appear to be as popular in the African country as they are back home. (A.B. Cross)

Brand new RTL1514 from Chalk Farm garage is parked rather awkwardly on the stand at Camden Gardens looking rather as if it has just been driven down from the garage. How nice these buses looked before they received advertisements and 1954 was to be the last year any could be regularly observed in this state as new deliveries ceased. (W. Legg)

The two LGOC built STL1 type bodies which had been fitted along with new and other earlier examples to the "unfrozen" new AEC chassis delivered in 1941/42 still remained in use as staff buses in 1954. STL2679 is shown elsewhere in this book but here at Chiswick Works on 27th October at the end of its days, STL2674 has strangely assumed a little more of the appearance the body would have had when originally fitted to STL200 in 1933. The reason is that it has somehow acquired the smaller radiator and registration plate from STL537. (J.C. Gillham)

On 17th March Camberwell garage gained a Sunday allocation of eight buses on route 45 which, since its introduction to replace Tram 34, had been the sole preserve of Clapham garage. On the 11th April RTL1482 stands at the Elephant & Castle working a short journey between there and Battersea, Parkgate Road. (W. Legg)

STL1743, a 4/9STL11 variant, which is depicted elsewhere in this book working one of its last duties on route 93, stands to the right of STL505, a 2/16STL18, both sadly awaiting their fate while parked within the expanse of Fulwell depot in April. Lurking in the background a Q type trolleybus with blinds set for route 667 stands just inside the depot. Eventually the trolleybus together with the higher numbered of the STLs would be exported for further service. (J. Gascoine collection)

GS75 was initially in store at Garston garage along with the majority of the last sixteen or so of this small class of 84 vehicles until suitable work could be found for them. Happily not too many months were spent idle as the vehicle was put to work in the summer. It is seen here on the Rickmansworth stand of the short 361 route to Chorleywood through Heronsgate and The Swillet which was converted from operation by a crewed T to a one-man GS on May 19th. (R.H.G. Simpson)

RT4507 photographed at the Minories bus station, Aldgate while laying over before commencing a further journey on the 723A route to Grays. The 723 group of Green Line routes had lost their RF coaches in favour of RT buses on 7th July which, while providing more capacity, albeit at a reduced frequency, was hardly a positive step in terms of comfort for the passengers. At the same time the 723A route, which deviated through the Aveley Estate, was cut back to Grays from Tilbury Ferry. (Roy Marshall)

Seen here at Ascot, Craven bodied RT1476 in red livery operates the special race meeting service from Staines. The usual British summer has left a rather muddy area which the bus driver has found convenient to park in. In the middle distance to the left of the picture a board proclaims "Buses for Reading" for which the queue of people are presumably waiting.

6½ ton overhead wire lubricator 422W was once T306, numerically the last of the early Green Line coaches which were replaced later by the famous 9T9 and 10T10 types. T306 served the London Transport trolleybus network in this guise from March 1940 through to August 1952 and the vehicle is seen here after its disposal two years later in the yard of Lammas Motors in south-west London. Running repairs to the engine of a van, which appears to have lost its spare wheel, are being carried out. The car in the background carries a tyreless spoked spare wheel, not much good if a puncture were to ensue and a Bedford lorry together with motor bike complete the picture. (A.B. Cross)

RTW78 and RTW41 wait outside the Eagle at Ladbroke Grove on the 8th May while a mangy dog investigates a possible meal in the gutter. Both vehicles now operate out of Upton Park garage, the lower numbered having seen previous service from Alperton and Tottenham garages while RTW78 had only previously operated from Shepherds Bush. (J.H. Aston)

The interior of Addlestone garage with red STL2392 standing next to RT3622 and, just in view, RLH48 recently transferred in from Amersham. The STL resided at this garage for nearly six months before finally being transferred as a trainer to Muswell Hill and then Enfield garage after which it was despatched to Norths for scrap. (J. Gascoine collection)

STL1038 started life as a front entrance 10STL6 with LPTB bodywork, receiving a rear entrance variety of body in June 1948. It is pictured here inside Chiswick Works on 17th March with its final fitted body, an STL14 variety, number 16966. The bus was later to be operated by D. Bayliss of Creca near Gretna Green and must have been a fine addition to their fleet when one considers its age and neat appearance in this photograph. (J.C. Gillham)

New Monday – Saturday route 801 was introduced on the 3rd March to run from Stevenage Railway Station to Shephall, Valley Way, a newly built area, using one RT from Hitchin garage. RT3723 is seen here outside the old station buildings, now demolished and replaced by a new station nearer the Town Centre. The bus had been in service for around twelve months at different garages but is still devoid of any outside advertising. (P.J. Marshall)

Country Area bus RF611 is pressed into service as GF76 on Green Line route 715. Seen in Central London the vehicle still has around another 35 miles to go before completing its journey from Hertford. The passengers might not have noticed any difference until they tried to put their luggage on the rack and sat down on the seats. (R. Marshall)

The date is the 21st March and TD54 operating from Hornchurch garage carries a light load while on route 252 the long standing Romford service. In 1954 the route was still at its nadir, trundling between the station and Birch Road, a journey of only 9 minutes duration. Later in the year the bus would receive its second overhaul and be returned to service from Edgware garage, its first transfer since initial delivery to Hornchurch in January 1949. Another picture in this book shows it in its new home. (A.B. Cross)

Battersea garage only played host to RTL502 for a couple of months during 1954. Having arrived from Camberwell it moved into Dalston soon after this photograph was taken, so an outing on route 31 to Camden Town Station did not happen often, particularly since the normal allocation was of RTWs. The destination blind with its admonition of "ONLY" belongs to route 39 since route 31 had not ventured beyond Camden Town since 1917. (A.B. Cross)

Squeezed in between STL1706 and RT4099, RT4473 had only just been transferred to Addlestone garage, having spent its first few months in service in the Central Area at Twickenham garage. The red liveried STL at the time was a Grays vehicle while RT4099 normally resided at Guildford. The Ascot race meeting was the occasion for Special Service 443 to operate. (J. Gascoine Collection)

STD83 put in nearly a year's work as a trainer after it had finished its revenue earning days in June, the last month of passenger operation of these 1STD1s. It is seen here running down the A23 working from distant Southall which was the first garage to use it in this capacity before it later moved to Stockwell and Norbiton. Following behind the STD is Ford's final attempt to make its pre-war 10hp. model look modern. The last "sit up and beg" Prefect in this form was produced from 1948 to 1953 when it was succeded by the slab sided Prefect 100E. Note the Pilot model look-alike front on the car which was so un-aerodynamic that it actually reduced its m.p.g. capability. (Roy Marshall)

North Street garage began to lose their small allocation of SRTs in April in favour of RTs. SRT33, immaculate from its earlier overhaul and complete with a full set of route blinds, operates on route 66 and is seen at Romford. The body found its way on to the chassis of RT4468 at Chiswick works in July and the new bus then saw service at Forest Gate garage which was also involved at the time in operating route 66.

At the close of the year only the last batch of 20 STLs, delivered after the war in the early months of 1946, would be left operational from the once largest class owned by the LPTB. All twenty were originally operated by Watford High Street garage but towards the end of their career with the Executive many had moved eastwards to Grays or Hertford. Those at Hertford were specifically for route 327 which had a bridge with a weight restriction en route which precluded the use of post-war RTs. Here STL2683 stands in Hertford bus station accompanied by parked cars of Vauxhall, Morris and Austin manufacture. These sub-class 18STL20s never exchanged bodies, but one interesting fact was that this bus was originally painted red, as were two others of the batch, being repainted into Country Area green some few months after delivery.

The annual ritual of the Epsom Derby day in 1954 saw many fairly new vehicles in evidence and here RT4487 closely followed by RT4484 helps with the movement of the crowds. The fare from the Downs to the Town Station was 6d as indicated by the very basic fare table which can be seen in the lower saloon. (J. Gascoine Collection)

The two photographs of a Duple bodied six-wheel coach and the two 1930 photographs of LT1000 when new seem to bear little relationship other than the registration number GF7254. They are however the same vehicle. The chassis was built by the London General Omnibus Company as one of a small number of experimental six-wheeled vehicles. The type never went into full scale production being overtaken by the AEC Renown. Originally the vehicle was built utilising a petrol engine by Henry Meadows Ltd. of Wolverhampton. When licensed on the 31st July 1930 it carried an open driver's cab and had a protruding radiator with "General" inscribed at the top. The body was an LGOC double deck 54 seat example, similar to the then current style on LT type buses with an enclosed platform and straight staircase. A standard AEC petrol engine replaced the rather longer than usual Meadows variety in October 1933 and the bus was disposed of by London Transport in May 1939. (A.B. Cross)

White Heather Coaches of Southsea operated the vehicle when rebuilt as a coach for many years and it is seen here at South Parade Pier in Southsea on the 10th September making a striking contrast to its former appearance. (J.C. Gillham)

The pleasant greenery of the southernmost remnants of Epping Forest provides the backdrop for STD114 while driver and conductor have a friendly chat in this view taken on the 14th August. The last survivors of the STD class, which originally totalled 176, would still be in daily service at the turn of the year and indeed Loughton garage would not experience RT operation until 1955. The 20A was a new daily route from Leytonstone introduced on 19th May by extending the Loughton garage short workings on route 20 through the Debden estate to Debden Station, which in turn allowed the 167 to take the more direct route along Rectory Lane. (J.H. Aston)

Stockwell garage, opened in 1952, was the last garage to receive an allocation of the post-war STD type of vehicle for operational purposes. STD122, one of the many transferred in from Victoria when the 77 route was reallocated to this garage, stands at Kings Cross while waiting to commence a further journey to the Mitre at Tooting. Not the best of rides would be provided in this area of the Capital as evidenced by the road surface provided. (Roy Marshall)

RTW266 is a strange visitor to route 85 on 15th August. At this time the route was officially allocated RTs. The rogue vehicle stands in the sun at Putney Bridge Station, the long standing northern terminus of the route to Kingston. (J.H. Aston)

The author always thought that the use of full blinds on a bus with cream upper deck window surrounds looked more attractive than when carried on a bus in the newer all red colour scheme. Here, at Camberwell Green opposite its home garage of Walworth on the 14th January, RTL766 pauses on its way from the Embankment to Brockley. At the end of the year in December the bus will be overhauled and repainted, losing this appealing livery in the process. (A.B. Cross)

Back in 1948 Boughton's Service Station Ltd. of London E2 was one of the coach operators who provided vehicles and drivers to supplement London bus routes. In 1954 however they owned what was once tunnel STL1861 which they had acquired in October 1953 from Victoria Coaches of Leigh on Sea. The bus now looks very smart against a background of decaying double deckers, waste and scrap in the yard of this east London operator. The telephone numbers are a nostalgic reminder of the days when the name of the exchange meant something and you didn't need to memorise ten or more digits.

Building and works contractors have always been able to find further work for buses and coaches once their use as PSVs is over. Here what was STL1647 in the Executive's fleet heads a line-up of various vehicles including single deck EEP901 and a lowbridge double decker.

Photographed in June at Beaconsfield, this full frontal view of GS64 shows to good advantage the well proportioned bodywork to the adapted truck front end that was utilised in the construction of these one man operated buses. The route 373 was operated by Amersham garage and like so many GS routes was previously operated by a member of the C class. (A.B. Cross)

Standing among the trees at Putney Heath waiting to return to Camden Town on the Zoo bus route 74, RTW396 gives a good impression of the craftsmanship of the work force of Aldenham that could be seen when a bus left after receiving an overhaul. This example had received such attention in the previous month of July. (J.H. Aston)

All the B class of 29 vehicles found work with new operators after disposal by the Executive. Here what was once B29 plies for passengers in Brighton having been purchased by Brighton, Hove and District and allocated their fleet number 5999. In 1955 the small batch of four vehicles purchased would receive new ECW bodywork, their original austerity Duple examples being scrapped. (J. Gascoine Collection)

Kingston Station terminus provides the resting place for Norbiton garage's T724 in company with RT1439 on 20th June. 264 was the highest numbered Central Area daytime bus route in 1954. Both buses are serving Walton but after crossing Kingston Bridge the single decker will keep north of the River Thames until Walton Bridge while the double decker will cross Hampton Court Bridge and the two will meet in Walton from opposite directions. (J.H. Aston)

For some time the short 129 route had been the responsibility of Upton Park garage but on 3rd February the allocation was transferred to Seven Kings who operated RTLs. RTL383 stands at the Ilford terminus on 21st February displaying its very clear blind which fails to inform anyone that the route actually runs via Barkingside. Someone in a hurry to reach Claybury Broadway would have been better advised to catch a 144 which ran straight up Woodford Avenue. (A.B. Cross)

Brand new RTL1503 passes by some very undesirable property in the Chalk Farm area on its way to Pimlico, Grosvenor Road on the 18th May. Route 24 was converted from SRT class operation during the year under review. (W. Legg)

Green Line route 720A to Harlow New Town from Aldgate commenced operation on 30th June and RF120 is seen at the Minories Bus and Coach Station with the now 12 years old staff canteen still occupying its site in the far corner. The destination blind provided was unusual in not showing a via point on what, although an off-shoot of 720, was still a route of reasonable length. (J. Gascoine Collection)

C91 was withdrawn from service in December of the previous year and is seen here waiting its eventual sale to W. North in July parked alongside a trolleybus. During the year the last of these delightful one man operated 20 seater Leyland Cub buses were withdrawn from service. The production run of vehicles used the Leyland KPO3 chassis, the O indicating an oil engine being fitted, and were delivered in 1935 and 1936, the first seventy-four for the Country Area. The second batch, of which 91 was one, were bodied by Weymann and these were allocated to the Central Area. Over the years some of these were repainted green and this example finished life as a Country Area bus being last used at Epping garage. (Lens of Sutton)

This bus was once D10 in the London fleet but now it is operating for Transport Motor Services of Bishop Auckland. During the year platform doors would be added but the standard London Transport fitted garage and running number plate holders were kept, a distinguishing feature which often draws attention to the London origins of secondhand vehicles around the world. (R.F. Mack)

Although route number 423 had been converted to RT operation in 1952, red STL2358, a 4/9STL14/1 works as DT53 to the Dartford football ground. A few of the STL class were operated by this garage practically right up to the last day of operation of the type. (J.G.S. Smith collection)

Not usually associated with this class, Dalston garage has put SRT83 to good use on the long haul route 47 from Shoreditch to Farnborough. Many of the passengers seem to have recognised that they are having their picture taken and look directly at the cameraman but no doubt they are unaware that they are sitting in an unusual vehicle for both the garage and the route. They may however think the engine tone a little odd when the bus gets going! (J. Gascoine Collection)

One of the occupants of Edgware garage yard on 15th July is STL1765 which has obviously been involved in a decapitation accident. Where or when is unknown but since it was a Hitchin vehicle one wonders whether someone had tried to drive it into the actual garage which could only accommodate single deckers. (J.H. Aston)

"To and From Lords" slip boards are carried by RT682 and the following RT as they wait to commence their journeys on route 113 to Oxford Circus from Edgware. In the background withdrawn STDs from the first batch await their fate. RT682 was the unlucky vehicle which lost its roof in Twyford Abbey Road when being delivered new from Park Royal Coachworks in 1948. (A.B. Cross)

Nine days before withdrawal STL1743 works an unusual short journey on route 93 from Epsom to North Cheam, Queen Victoria and is seen here in Epsom town centre on 21st April. In the background RT1068 runs short to Epsom on the Kingston – Redhill route 406. This suggests it may be a race meeting day and the conductor has made good use of the hybrid blind layout to emphasise the working. STLs were not usual on the 93 route at this late date. Just overtaking the STL is one of the comparatively rare convertible versions of Issigonis's Morris Minor Series MM. Its traditional Morris grill and plain chrome strip above the Morris emblem show that it was manufactured in 1952 at the latest and has the original Morris 918cc side valve engine. (L.T.P.S.)

Seen at Teddington on the 19th April having just returned to service after its initial overhaul, RTL556 carries a Metro Cammell all metal body distinguishable by the narrower cream strip with prominent beading. Although the bus is working through to Highgate it carries a route blind specially designed for short workings on route 27 from Hammersmith to Teddington. In the following month this RTL would be transferred to Clapham garage. (J.H. Meredith)

After several promises route 94 was finally extended at its southern end beyond Southborough to Petts Wood Station on 19th May. Craven bodied RT1518 waits, presumably for a fresh crew from Catford garage, at Grove Park Station blinded for the weekend extension beyond Lewisham to Brockley Rise. (W. Legg)

On 4th January, the day before the demise of Nunhead garage, RT1459 stands with one of its colleagues from that shed, both displaying a destination that was to disappear from London route blinds. Something strange seems to have happened to the brickwork behind the bus! (A.B. Cross)

Older examples of the STL class in the shape of 548 and 1840 saw service to the last day of operation on the 31st August. Interestingly both are in Central Area livery, being used at Hitchin on the 303 and 392 group of routes which were Stevenage New Town and works services. The "To Town Tonight" advert obviously remains from its allocation to Hounslow and was of little use to the inhabitants of North Hertfordshire. (J. Gascoine Collection)

The ever changing scene around Piccadilly Circus in the heart of London can be clearly appreciated when this picture is compared to those shown in the 1948 and 1949 books of this series. Every bus passing through this famous tourist area of the capital is now of the RT family, although in this picture none can be positively identified. The County Fire Office in the middle of the background, which is designed to dominate the view up Lower Regent Street, was rebuilt to the design of Sir Reginald Blomfield in the twentieth century although it still carries the 1807 date of its predecessor designed by Royal Architect John Nash. (London Transport U56853)

Enfield garage was only associated with pre-war STDs in their latter days and even then it was their real home garage of Hendon which had the honour of operating the very last. Here one of the Enfield emigrants, STD47, works route 107 at Oakwood Station before the route had been extended beyond Borehamwood to Queensbury, absorbing the 141 in the process, on 3rd February. The 107 route was re-stocked with RTs and after that the STDs were confined to weekday work on the 107A at the eastern end of this long cross-North London route. Enfield's last STD was withdrawn on 30th April. (D.A. Ruddom collection)

STL1760 picture in its last throes as a passenger vehicle operating from Chalk Farm garage on route 24 in March, substituting for an SRT. It stands outside the Delco Remy premises at Pimlico while awaiting a return journey to Hampstead Heath. (J. Gascoine collection)

Kingsbury Square at Aylesbury provides the stand for RT606 and a couple of Thames Valley Bristol Ks in an era long since gone with town improvements over many years. The London bus has a healthy load of passengers seated and waiting the departure for a journey which will use the trunk A41 road between the town and its eventual destination at Watford Junction. (R.H.G. Simpson)

RT3091 looks a little in need of a freshen up as it pulls in at Catford while working route 124. Four years work from Catford garage seems to have had an unduly bad effect on the paintwork. (A.B. Cross)

The wide expanse of Wandsworth Common provides a pleasant, if wintry, background to Battersea's RTL360 as it heads for Upper Tooting (Tooting Bec Station) on Route 19. The rather strange name of Tooting Bec comes from the Benedictine Abbey of St. Mary of Bec in Normandy who held this land at the time of the Domesday Survey and whose Abbot set up a gallows in Tooting Bec in 1258. All of which has nothing to do with RTL360 as it pursues its mundane task!
(C. Carter)

RT99 first appeared at Chiswick works on the 24th January 1940 and is now seen fourteen years later at Golders Green Station in the company of its post-war sisters including RT1302, full blinded but with cream upper deck window surrounds and very shortly to be overhauled. Route 28 first received an allocation of these vehicles in March 1940 only to lose them in favour of STs in November of that year. Then from 1941 to 1947 Putney garage withdrew in favour of Battersea but on 12th November 1947 AF again returned and the 2RT2 remained a familiar sight on the route until their replacement by RTLs in 1955.

All the Lanes and Greens which Route 204 passes on its way from Uxbridge to Hayes, as shown on the blind, make one realise what a delightful place rural Middlesex must have been before the inexorable spread of suburbia made RT1903's journey a very mundane affair. The sunshine of the 4th July is enjoyed by the crew in the entrance to the Bus Station at Uxbridge. (J.H. Aston)

The first example of AEC Regals numbered in the T class entered service in November 1929 with bodywork built by the London General Omnibus Company at their Chiswick works. They were built for bus work and had rear platform type bodies with seating for 30 passengers. One vehicle of the batch of 50, T38, was given a Green Line coach body and to compensate T156 was provided with a bus body but this had a front entrance and was the very first such example in the General fleet. 1930 saw the rebuilding of T27 to front entrance configuration which became the second such vehicle in the fleet. In 1931 five of these buses, T15, 21, 25, 26 and 35 were handed over to the East Surrey Traction Co. Ltd. together with the Crayford garage and these buses passed to London General Country Services in 1932 eventually being repainted into County Area green on the formation of the LPTB. In the period 1933 through to 1935 the remaining 43 vehicles still in red livery were rebuilt to the front entrance layout. The photographs shown on these two pages show T31 on the 14th July at the driver training school within Chiswick Works complete with a CS garage plate. It appears to have gained a strange all over red livery with black band at roof level. Thankfully the bus was saved for preservation when disposed of by the Executive in October 1956 and was eventually rebuilt into its original condition and has been admired by enthusiasts at many rallies. The two colour prints show the bus at the Golden Jubilee Celebrations of London Transport. A fine tribute to everyone who had the foresight and enthusiasm to see the task through of saving this particular vehicle for posterity. (J.C. Gillham) (colour prints D.A. Ruddom)

This bus is thought to be Q103 of the 1/4Q4/1 variety and is seen at Birhara, Malta, in company with another veteran vehicle possibly of Reo manufacture operating on the service from Valetta. The Q had first been shipped to Malta for the movement of workers employed by McAlpine, the civil engineering group engaged in the reconstruction of the bomb damaged Malta dockyards. When the work was nearing completion the opportunity was taken to dispose of the vehicle and an enterprising local operator quickly realised its potential. A more modern and flamboyant grill in place of the London Transport square example adds individuality to the bus. (B. Burrell)

Originally G204 but now Highland Omnibus of Inverness fleet number E88, the chassis of this vehicle would be rebuilt and rebodied later in the year with a single deck body. Here however it is in much the same condition as when operating in London. Somehow the passengers must know they are on the right bus but strangers to the locality might not have been so sure since there seems to be a complete absence of route information.

Green liveried STL1680 was parked up at Edgware awaiting its destiny at the same time as STL1765, which is shown elsewhere in this book. Eventually the bus was despatched to W. North the dealers near Leeds in June 1955. Hertford garage was the last operational home of this 4/9STL14. (J.H. Aston)

This was once STL719 and is now Leon Motor Services Ltd. of Finningley number 33. The bus was photographed on the 1st September just two months after being acquired by its new operator from W. North of Leeds, the dealer who at the time was taking most of the time expired London vehicles. The vehicle is seen at Waterdale in Doncaster with a Corporation owned AEC Regent III with Roe bodywork, fleet number 128, which entered service during the year under review. (R. Holmes)

The Green Line standby vehicle kept at Victoria garage for use in the event of a Green Line breakdown within Central London was, for a few months in 1954, T639. The front blind box is restricted to show only a one line destination display so that the long blind needed to contain all the routes could be accommodated.

The tram replacement route 70 was extended on 17th March from Greenwich to Eltham and from Waterloo to Victoria via Lambeth Bridge. Previously on 6th January the allocation had been moved from Peckham, to New Cross and one of that garage's 2RT2s, RT96, stands at Victoria Station. Nothing has been done it seems to add the 70 route to the bus stop it shares with route 10 on the station forecourt. (J. Gascoine Collection)

Bickers of Coddenham in Suffolk acquired ex T300 from Osborne of Tollesbury after the latter concern had had it rebodied with a new Duple 32 seat coach body as depicted here. The coach had been sold by the Board to Arlington Motor Company of London SW1 in August 1938 having first entered service in February 1931 and it was to continue in service until March 1959.

Excursion number 8 was a new facility introduced for the 1954 season and ran from Blackwall Tunnel to Hampton Court. Athol Street garaged RTL509 calls in at Aldgate Bus Station to see if there are any intending passengers at this pick-up point. (A.B. Cross)

Saunders bodied RT1331 was one of the vehicles exchanged by Willesden for Harrow Weald's short lived allocation of RTWs in 1951 and three years later it is still working HD's routes – in this case the 114 from Edgware to Rayners Lane. The neat little inspector's hut, complete with inspector inside, bears a similarity to the signal boxes you see today on some small gauge railways in parks and pleasure grounds. (A.B. Cross)

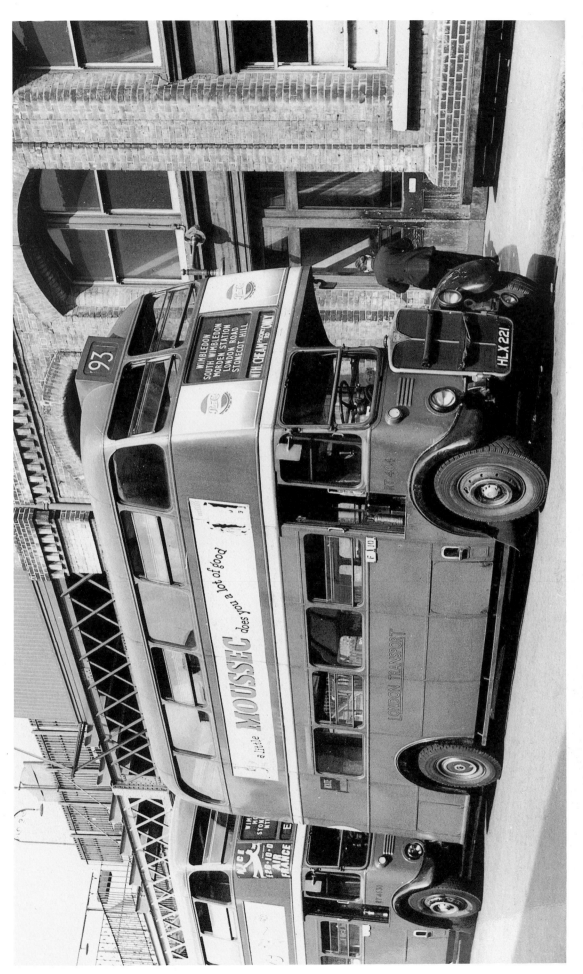

Photographed at Putney Bridge station waiting to commence a journey as far as Priory Road, North Cheam, RT404 carries a very early RT3 body fitted with a small offside route number holder to which the word "ROUTE" has been added on the black background when it was first overhauled in August 1951. By this time the short lived fashion of adding "ONLY" to short working destinations had ceased but this bus carries quite an old set of blinds compared to the vehicle behind. (J.H. Aston)

G436, the odd Guy Arab, continued to work from Enfield garage in 1954 on route 121, which at that time was a rather obscure shuttle across the Lea Valley. Here it leaves the garage forecourt on its route to Chingford which still involved traversing Alma Road and the level crossing at Ponders End Station. It was probably the latter obstacle which mitigated against any promotion of the service to more useful traffic objectives until the Lea Valley Road extension link to Nags Head Road was completed. (Lens of Sutton)

Taking a well earned rest, RT3633 stands alongside Victoria garage before returning south to Ascot as a Green Line relief from Staines garage. Route 701 appeared on 22nd June 1946 as an hourly service operating between Gravesend and Ascot via Victoria with the post-war reintroduction of the Green Line network. (P.J. Marshall)

The ex-London Guys pictured in previous books of this series continued to give good service at Melsbroek Airport in Belgium where this example is seen in July carrying registration number 521329 and fleet number 108. Any information on the Guys sold to Sabena in the early 50s would be welcomed by the author. Obviously a Weymann bodied product, this vehicle could be ex-G405 which has been recorded with Sabena Airlines. (Sabena Belgian World Airlines)

In this line up on the 26th May at the Willesden Junction terminus in Honeywood Road, RTL928 from Shepherds Bush garage stands in front of RT3358 from Rye Lane garage. RL had taken over the duties on the 12 route from Nunhead when the latter garage closed on the night of 5th/6th January. The route operated in two sections, the northern part shown here only running as far as Dulwich. To complete the line-up is a Ford Pilot, on the market from 1947 until 1951, being the only post war version of the famous Ford V8 with astonishingly poor all round operating performance from its 3622cc engine. (J.H. Aston)

Hendon's STD92 advertises Three Threes cigarettes at 10 for 1/9½d, which in today's money equates to approximately 9p. Prices for the smoker have certainly changed! This view is taken at the Post Office in North Harrow on the 23rd January. Next door to the Post Office is a 3d lending library with "thousands of books to choose from", an enterprise long since disappeared but bearing a similarity to the video lending shops of today. (J.C. Gillham)

Upton Park's RTW78 heads west into the evening sunlight to Ladbroke Grove, The Eagle. At the shop on the right you could have your picture taken by Polyfoto, "the Natural Photographer". This did not mean in the nude but rather you would receive a sheet of lots of passport sized pictures of yourself looking in all directions from which those of your choice could be enlarged. (R.F. Mack)

Another red STL to complete its service with the Executive in the Country Area was STL2086. Here in Hertford bus station it waits in stand 6 reserved for routes 327, 389 and 399. Body number 97 first mounted on STL2566 appears to be in good order. (J.G.S. Smith Collection)

STL1784 still has to make one more garage transfer to Hertford which allowed the bus to continue in service up to the last day of operation of STLs in the Country Area. Here in the company of an RT it waits to start its journey to Sidcup Station from Horton Kirby on route 467. (J. Gascoine collection)

This photograph of RF39 clearly shows the absence of a horizontal passenger safety rail on the nearside front window. Although later delivered vehicles of the class were fitted with the rail when new, earlier variants were only modified subsequently. The coach is seen climbing Thames Street in historic Windsor as it nears the end of a long haul from Tunbridge Wells. (J. Fozard)

RTL452, another bus fitted with traffic arm indicators, stands at the Crystal Palace terminus of route 108 on the 27th August. No longer are special vehicles considered necessary on the Blackwall Tunnel route, although this Athol Street bus will have been fitted with tyres having reinforced walls to cope with rubbing against the kerb in the narrow roadway. (J.H. Aston)

RTL82 seen on the 8th May while operating the short-lived route 5 which ran between Ladbroke Grove, St. Charles Square and Shepherds Bush Green until it was withdrawn on the 19th May due to poor patronage. The picture was taken at St. Charles Square as the bus was being followed by a Triumph saloon, introduced in 1946 as the 1800 and later with enlarged engine of 2000cc as the Renown – shades of AEC! A real gentleman's car in true English tradition, it was known as "The Top Hat". (J.H. Aston)

One time STL2232 in the London Transport fleet, having been acquired by Hants and Sussex in 1953, now stands unwanted in 1954 after its new operator finally ceased operations. The LPTB built lowbridge body clearly shows the cut out of the upper structure above the rear platform allowing easy access to the saloons. From that point onwards however taller passengers had to be aware of the lower ceilings. First put into service in September 1937 the vehicle originally was a highbridge example, receiving its new lowbridge body in March 1943. To which part of the Littlewoods empire does the rear end advertisement relate? The bus was finally scrapped at the Brooklyn Engineering Works at Chandlers Ford in Hampshire in October.

Pictured arriving at Hertford Bus Station, RF573 working from Hertford garage, looks as though it has encountered some muddy road conditions. The blinds are set for a trip to Little Berkhampstead, as it was then spelt, on route 308A, which should mean a fairly easy job for the conductor who can just be seen with his Bell Punch. The 308A was part of the large group of single deck routes emanating from Hertford whose schedules were interworked between Hertford, Epping and Hitchin garages and included the 384 to Letchworth, the 399 to Coopersale as well as the 308 to Cuffley. The crews needed a pretty good knowledge of rural Hertfordshire. (M. Rooum)

One man operation of larger single deck vehicles got under way from March with the introduction into service of RF517, 647 and 700 on route 419. The modifications deemed necessary on these vehicles were much greater than on later conversions and are shown in this interior view of RF647. Note the shortened nearside longitudinal seat with small luggage pen, the wider driver's cab with sloping lower area, the interior rear view mirror above the front nearside windscreen and "pay as you enter" sign just visible at the top. Two Ultimate ticket machines mounted side by side on the inside of the open driver's door with cash and ticket trays above and time card holder below can be seen and although not very clear in this picture, a full height glass screen on the door with "speak" hole. (A.B. Cross)

Rain soaked Dumfries reveals Western SMT Guy Arab II, fleet number DY1054, once London Transport G178, having been rebodied with a secondhand 1947 built Croft low height body originally mounted on Leyland TD1 registration TM3846. The Leyland vehicle had been acquired by Western SMT when they took over the Caledonian Omnibus Company of Dumfries in January 1950. (Ian Maclean)

The former Festival of Britain service from South Kensington to Battersea Park was numbered 45A for the 1954 season and on the 8th May Clapham's RTL1076 heads for the Festival Gardens. Despite the bright sunshine there are as yet not many interested parties in such a day out but judging by the shadows it is still early in the day. (A.B. Cross)

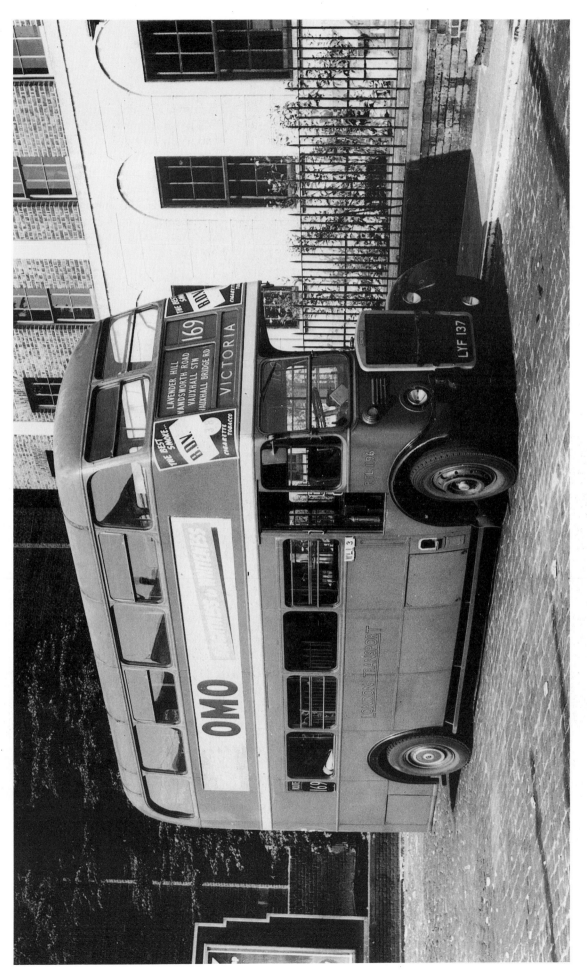

RTL1196 rests on the stand in the forecourt of the British Railway Stores office in St. Johns Hill at Clapham Junction before its return journey to Victoria. The attractive premises, complete with garden railing, belie their prosaic use. The Sunday allocation for this former tram route was transferred from Camberwell garage across the road to Walworth starting on 25th July and this shows the new order in operation three weeks later. (J.H. Aston)

Long before Riverdale Centres or even Bus Stations were thought about at Lewisham, RT555, a Catford bus since delivery in June 1948, stands in the damp surroundings of Rennell Street. The number 1 bus route can trace its ancestry to the Vanguard Service from Brondesbury to Law Courts which was extended in August 1905 to run from Cricklewood to Elephant & Castle. Strange that the first number should evolve into a relatively backwater route in inner south east London while the glamorous roads are left to higher numbers. (A.B. Cross)

The once important route from Victoria to Ilford, Barkingside and Chigwell Row had commenced in February 1921 as 25B. It was renumbered under the "Bassom Scheme" to 26, renumbered 25A when "Bassom" ceased, lost its London end in the Second World War cutbacks and was renumbered 26 again in 1948. It then gradually dwindled away since it followed the old route up Fencepiece Road and along Manor Road whereas new route 150 ran from Ilford to Chigwell Row through the heart of the new Hainault estate. By 1954 just four buses from Seven Kings garage were sufficient for the 26 and on 21st February RTL423 was the second of the four for the day. Two patient passengers await departure from Ilford. (A.B. Cross)

The Peckham – Nunhead circular route 173 was still operated by Nunhead on Mondays to Fridays when that garage closed after 5th January. After that Peckham would replace Nunhead on those days but in turn would lose their Sunday duties to Rye Lane. RT1545 is seen at the beginning of the year making up one of the six vehicles required for the Nunhead duties on this local route. It would be transferred to North Street, Romford once its present home closed. (J. Gascoine collection)

Photographed at High Beach in the heart of Epping Forest, RF25 and RF7 make an impressive sight as they sit beneath the green foliage. Is there a problem or are the drivers fixing up one of those roulette lotteries on the rear wheel beloved of coach drivers on outings at the time? (C. Carter)

All of the 5Q5 variety of buses were disposed of by London Transport to W. North the well known dealer from Leeds and a few were then exported and saw further service in such unlikely places as Cyprus, Rangoon, Tripoli and Malta. Here one, which saw further service in Cyprus operating for the Famagusta Bus Service, is seen in the new town area of Famagusta known as Varosha. It brought a tinge of homesickness to one National Service Airman on leave from the Canal Zone! (D. A. Ruddom)

For two years after sale by the Executive former STL765 could still be seen on the streets of London operated by Valliant Direct Coaches Ltd. of W5. Seen here in Tavistock Road, Harlesden, devoid of all ownership details and looking a little sad for itself, it would, in the following year, be despatched to a London dealer for scrap. (A.B. Cross)

GS74, one of just over a dozen put into store when new, having been delivered in early 1954, after work had been found for it later in the year. It is seen here at Hertford bus station operating the rural route 388 with a fabulous array of parked cars in the background. Included is an Austin 10 Litchfield, a pre-war Flying Standard 14 and, sideways on, an Austin Hereford A70 first introduced in the Autumn of 1951 to be replaced in 1954 by the A90 Westminster.

The bridge over the lines to Morden Underground Depot and the familiar totem form the background to this picture of RT1491 and RT4654 as they stand in the Morden Station forecourt on the 27th February. The bus nearer the camera had received its first overhaul in November of the previous year while the other is new to the rigours of everyday life in London having been first put to use in January of this year. The 157 is working a short journey to Hackbridge. (A.B. Cross)

On 3rd July nineteen year old STL900 is still looking sprightly at Garston as it works what appears to be an additional duty on route 318. This would be its final month in service although it would not be disposed of to W. North until the following March. (G. Mead)

The date is the 13th July and there is still evidence of wartime bomb damage in London as here at Finsbury Square. RT776 would appear to have been taken out of service for some reason as the running number stencil has been removed, route 43 offside plate turned outside down and the intermediate blind wound to "Private", a necessity before the days of "Sorry Not in Service" whenever a vehicle broke down. (J.H. Aston)

Somebody at Dalston garage has made a start on converting RT690 to a full blind display but the work has not made a lot of progress. The timekeeper at the Kings Arms, Peckham Rye, seems happy with life although with Nunhead garage due to close at the end of the duties on the following day, regulation at this point on the route is not likely to be required after that. (A.B. Cross)

A fine study in the frontal treatment given to ex-D274 while owned by the Executors of S. Ledgard of Leeds, who operated the bus in the years 1953 through to 1960. The front upper deck opening windows have been replaced by non-opening panes, while the three piece route destination arrangement has been replaced by a single oblong opening. The dimensions of the original display can be discerned with the beading still in place above and a line of rivet heads at the bottom holding the replacement panel in place. The radiator surround has either been replaced or burnished to gleam in a manner never seen while the vehicle was operating in London. (R.L. Kell/A.B. Cross)

When new, RT3725 enjoyed a short spell in operation at Windsor and then was stored at Garston garage until its re-entry into service in 1954 from Hitchin garage. This explains the lack of advertising, which might otherwise have detracted from the apparent newness of the bus although it is already over twelve months old. Here it stands in Guildhouse Street beside Victoria garage awaiting return to Hitchin via the northern half of route 716 on a Green Line relief duty. (A.B. Cross)

Victoria garage had a Sundays only allocation on route 24 and Craven bodied RT1490 lays over at five to one on a Sunday lunchtime at South End Green, Hampstead Heath. The time is ascertained from that indispensable piece of London Transport roadside furniture of the period, the time clock. Presumably the lock has failed on this one since it has been propped open. All 120 of the Craven bodied RTs received an overhaul in their fairly short life with London Transport and this bus had received one in November 1953. In May 1956 together with a number of others of the type, it received Country Area colours before being disposed of to Birds the dealers at Stratford-upon-Avon. The posters are evocative of the fifties. Billy Daniels is making his farewell appearance at the Chiswick Empire and Eagle Steamers are offering day cruises to the sea and French coast cruises from Gravesend for 21/-. (J. Gascoine collection)

On 30th June the short 147 route which ran from Redbridge Station to Ilford via The Drive was extended through new territory via Little Ilford Lane and Browning Road to East Ham and onwards in peak hours to Royal Albert Docks and North Woolwich. Here Seven Kings' RTL224 stands at the White Horse, East Ham on the new extension. (W. Legg)

Standing under the shadows of wiring for trolleybus route 611 which shared the road from Highgate Village to here at the Archway Tavern, RF377 waits for a crew from the distant Muswell Hill garage before continuing its journey on route 210 to Wells Terrace at Finsbury Park. Seating for 41 passengers was provided on the Central Area variety of these underfloor engined AEC Regal Mark IV vehicles bodied by Metro Cammell. (P. Gomm collection)

A confused scene at the embryonic Stevenage Industrial Area as inspector and crew confer. T697 and STL2584 are working the 303 group of routes to Hitchin. The STL entered service in March 1939 as a 15STL16 and was repainted green in March 1941 along with others at the time. Its body, number 105, stayed matched to the chassis throughout its career with London Transport which ended in September when a pantechnicon body by Kean was mounted onto the chassis to form a removal lorry for Exeloak Furniture of London in January 1955. In the background of the picture can be seen an Austin Six with the word Six on its grille, a model on the market from 1932 to 1938.

Dartford garage was the last home for STL2021 before it was withdrawn from service and disposed of to W. North. The following year the bus was noted as a pantechnicon bodied furniture lorry with Exeloak Furniture of London but that is another story. Just now it is seen parked on some waste ground ready for service on route 423A before the type was expelled from all services operated by Dartford on the 11th August. (J. Gascoine Collection)

SRT32 operating from North Street, Romford garage at a very calm and peaceful "Green Man", Leytonstone stand before journeying to Hornchurch on route 66. On the 31st July RTs would take over the duties of the last remnants of this class at this garage together with the SRTs still operated by Forest Gate. These 160 hybrid vehicles had their fair share of problems with an under powered engine and difficulties with the braking system. The chassis for this vehicle came from STL2609 and the body was eventually used in the construction of RT4465. (P.J. Marshall)

By 1954 the former tram depots were beginning to become more integrated into the bus network. An example of this was the Sunday allocation introduced to route 37 on 6th January from Rye Lane and Clapham garages. Here Clapham's RTL827 passes a period British Home Stores next to a Scotch Wool Stores on its way to Richmond on 17th January. (A.B. Cross)

TD1, once a stable mate of TD24 seen elsewhere in this book, had already been transferred into Kingston garage in 1954. On the 18th April the bus stands at the back of the Kingston railway station bus terminus. Both the 1TD1s featured in this book ended their days in Ceylon as did so many of the class. (J.H. Aston)

The date is the 30th March and NLP635, the AEC Monocoach, having just arrived at Bromley by Bow, is working duty D3 on the 208. It will not be operating many more journeys on this route as it was returned to its owners, AEC Ltd. during the following month.

STL2693 was transferred from Grays garage to Hertford at the same time as the other example of this type shown elsewhere in this book. It is seen in deserted Hertford bus station waiting to take up duties on a short 327 working to Nazeing Gate. (J. Gascoine collection)

Premier Travel of Watford acquired ex T119 in September 1939 from a dealer by the name of Horne Products Ltd. of Colnbrook who had brought the coach from London Transport in July of the same year. During its operation by Premier the chassis was twice rebodied with new Thurgood coach examples and here in August, a month before being finally withdrawn from service, it is seen with the second body which seated 32 passengers. It stands between two other coaches while operating on a day trip to Margate. (P.S.A. Redmond)

RT1849 photographed on the 17th November at Clapham, carries route number 136 in all the right places and destination blind showing a fictitious 'St Johns Common'. For some years this unused number was reserved for filming and experimental purposes. The garage plate is a New Cross (NX) slipped into the holder upside down. All done in the name of realism for a scene to be used in the making of a film. (G. Mead)

All the four vehicles from London Transport Collection brought out for the Omnibus Society celebrations in this year are shown without apology within the pages of this book. Collectively they depict the early development of the petrol engined bus and their combined performance on 25th September was a highlight of 1954. The buses were greeted by considerable crowds at Piccadilly Circus. S742 first appeared on the streets of London in 1923 and the bus seated 54. Inside, firmly pasted and varnished on to the lower saloon ceiling, although not visible here of course, are posters extolling the Peahen Hotel at St. Albans, testimony to the vehicle's allocation to Hendon for work on route 84 in its latter days of service. (J.C. Gillham)

There was a symmetry about roofbox RTs with restricted blind displays that was always pleasing. This is well demonstrated by Leyton's RT1274 as it stands alongside one of the allegedly very cosy "prefabs" of the time. A youthful looking Billy Graham is about to conduct one of his evangelistic campaigns at Harringay Arena and admission is free. Did they have a collection I wonder? (A.B. Cross)

Riverside garage used their complement of RTWs on route 11 and here outside Broad Street Station the driver and conductress of RTW231 appear to be negotiating a short turn with an inspector before the blind is changed for the return journey. (J. Gascoine Collection)

T420 stands with STL1012 looking very weathered and forgotten in the scrapping fields of Vass of Ampthill, Beds. STL1012 is reported as having been inspected by a preservationist in 1951 but found unsuitable and returned to Vass. What a great pity as the bus would have been a highlight of rallies nowadays had its preservation been found to be economically viable.

Green liveried RT4476 spent its first four months of operational service at Central Area Twickenham garage and is seen here on route 90B while en route to Kew Gardens Station. Quite a number of similar liveried vehicles from the batch RT4473 to 4484 were put to service from this garage replacing SRT buses in the early months of the year and it was not until the summer that they found homes more suited to their colour scheme. It is perhaps ironic that the body carried by this "new" RT (number 4725) had previously been used on SRT71 although this was not one that had been allocated at Twickenham. (P.J. Marshall)

The street name signs clearly show where RTL357 is photographed in the heart of Camden Town. The run down atmosphere of the area is only broken by the appearance of the bus with its brightly finished paintwork having been recently overhauled. (A.B. Cross)

A further view of route 203 with STL1777 working duty AV2 at Twickenham Station while awaiting a return journey to Hatton Cross. Hounslow garage would be its last operational centre before becoming a staff bus. (J. Gascoine collection)

The RM class makes its debut in this series of books with RM1 appearing in public in September at the Commercial Motor Show. Here it stands outside the experimental department at Chiswick Works with Arthur Sainsbury (of STL2477 fame) walking past giving the bus his approving eye. Note the single line destination box above the platform and the one quite small aperture at the front of the vehicle. At the time this provoked much derogatory comment but the finished product in 1956 was equipped with the usual standard of London display. The new concept of flashing trafficators has also arrived and was to spread through the fleet rapidly in a few years time. Other interesting features are the lack of a conventional radiator grill and the quarter drop windows fitted which had last appeared on double deckers in London when a handful of 2RT2s incorporated them. There were many changes to be made before the bus finally appeared in service two years later. (J.C. Gillham)

AEC Monocoach NLP635 was returned to its rightful owners during the year along with the other experimental lightweight vehicles. D garage plates are still carried on the bus from its previous use by Dalston garage on route 208 as it stands in front of the licensing section building within the Chiswick Works complex on the 2nd March. (J.C. Gillham)

APPENDIX I

London Transport Central and Country Area Bus Garages

A	Sutton	J	Holloway
AB	Twickenham	K	Kingston
AC	Willesden	L	Loughton
AD	Palmers Green	LH*	Leatherhead
AE	Hendon	LS*	Luton
AF	Chelverton Road, Putney	M	Mortlake
AH	Nunhead	MA*	Amersham
AK	Streatham	MH	Muswell Hill
AL	Merton	N	Norwood
AM	Plumstead	NB	Norbiton
AP	Seven Kings	NF*	Northfleet
AR	Tottenham	NS	North Street, Romford
AV	Hounslow	NX	New Cross
AW	Abbey Wood	ON	Alperton
B	Battersea	P	Old Kent Road
BK	Barking	PB	Potters Bar
BN	Brixton	PM	Peckham
C	Athol Street, Poplar	Q	Camberwell
CA	Clapham	R	Riverside
CF	Chalk Farm	RD	Hornchurch
CL	Clay Hall	RE*	Romford, London Road
CM*	Chelsham	RG*	Reigate
CS	Chiswick (non-operational)	RL	Rye Lane
CY*	Crawley	S	Shepherds Bush
D	Dalston	SA*	St Albans
DG*	Dunton Green	SJ*	Swanley Junction
DS*	Dorking	SP	Sidcup
DT*	Dartford	ST*	Staines
E	Enfield	SW	Stockwell
ED	Elmers End	T	Leyton
EG*	East Grinstead	TB	Bromley
EP*	Epping	TC	Croydon
EW	Edgware	TG*	Tring
F	Putney Bridge	TH	Thornton Heath
G	Forest Gate	TL	Catford
GD*	Godstone	TW*	Tunbridge Wells
GF*	Guildford	U	Upton Park
GM	Gillingham Street, Victoria	UX	Uxbridge
GR*	Garston	V	Turnham Green
GY*	Grays	W	Cricklewood
H	Hackney	WA*	Watford, High Street
HD	Harrow Weald	WD	Wandsworth
HE*	High Wycombe	WG	West Green
HF*	Hatfield	WL	Walworth
HG*	Hertford	WR*	Windsor
HH*	Two Waters	WY*	Addlestone
HN*	Hitchin	X	Middle Row
HW	Southall	-	Aldenham (non-operational)

*indicates a Country Area garage.

The above list is of all operational garages plus the two main non-operational sites for bus maintenance available on 1st January 1953.

Only five days into the new year Nunhead garage was closed for operational purposes. At the time of closure buses were operating on routes 12, 37, 63 and 173, the work being reallocated to either Rye Lane or Peckham garages with other knock on effects. At the same time the use of the old Brixton Hill tram depot as a temporary overflow for Brixton garage ceased. During the year reconstruction work at Hornchurch, Shepherds Bush, Uxbridge and Walworth garages was completed.

APPENDIX II

Thanks to correspondence and more photographs from interested enthusiasts this Appendix is provided to enhance information in previously published books in this series.

1948 BOOK

Page 89   The bottom picture of STL2129 shows the bus when it was fitted with body number 17546 of STL15 type, an all metal framed body built by Park Royal. On closer examination it is apparent that the body has suffered bomb blast damage. Only one opening window per deck is now fitted, having originally been built with five on each side. A pre-war stencil holders is indented into the panel work above a newer additional wartime one. An older type nearside front mudguard unbalances the visual effect of the bus when compared to the correctly fitted offside fixture.

1950 BOOK

Almost unbelievable as it would first appear, closer examination of the bodywork reveals that this mobile travel bureau was once T288! Converted to normal control layout from its previous forward control configuration, it was photographed on 10th September 1950 at Dortmund in Germany with bomb scarred buildings as a backdrop. The bus had been disposed of to the War Department for Control Commission along with others at the end of World War II in Europe in May 1945 and was noted with a dealer in Iserlohn, West Germany as late as 1949. It is included here as an example of the ingenuity of man in turning something built for London usage into something so Continental looking. (J.C. Gillham)

1951 BOOK

Page 61   The lower picture is taken at the Wood Green Coach Station, frequented by Valiant of East London, Vineys of Tottenham and the lovely orange painted coaches of Grosvenor's. Standing just a few yards further along the road was the City Coach Company premises which were built in the early 1930s.

Page 101   The rebuilding of Marshall look-alike T30 at the top of the page was carried out at Chiswick Works over a period of several months between October 1949 and February 1950. Marshall rebuilds had been completed by the time T30 returned to service and it remains a mystery as to why this one off was picked to be rebuilt in this way. There were two main external differences on the bus; original rear light and number plate layout was retained and the offside valance above the windows was continued right up to the driver's cab.

1953 BOOK

Introduction RTC1 should be added to the list of withdrawn vehicles.

Page 20   The RF at the top of the page is pictured at the bus stop opposite Reigate garage. The "Desert Rat" public house further along Lesbourne Road is still in business to this day.

Page 81   Park Royal and Weymann manufactured bodies were built using 'Jicwood' one piece roofs between the domes. The external aluminium panels secured with rivets which had waterproofing fabric strips stuck in place with Bostic. Square shaped pieces of fabric were also applied to the roofs above the stanchion plates of all RT family vehicles except the RT8/2 variety. From 1953 towards the end of RT production Jicwood roofing was supplied in sections for new buses and in spare sections for the overhaul of the earlier members at Aldenham when at the same time metal strap plates were used as a replacement and stanchion plates were dispensed of together with the untidy fabric.

Page 106   The AEC Monocoach is pictured at the "Red Cross" stop in Reigate.

Page 130   The lower picture is in fact Two Waters bus garage and not Apsley Mills.

Page 148   STL1796 is pictured within the Leeds Central Bus Station, sometimes referred to as St. Peters Street Bus Station which opened in 1948 and which still functions basically on the same piece of land though contracted and expanded in various directions. The middle bus of the three in the background is BWR98 at Kippax and District. The owner of Burrows was a pigeon fancier and it was a regular sight when one of their buses arrived in Leeds Bus Station to see the conductor produce a basket of pigeons, check his watch and release the birds to fly back to their loft at Wombwell!

Appendix I   A note should have been included at the foot of the list of garages that Loughton garage closed and re-opened in new premises opposite the old on 2nd December 1953. The code remained unchanged as L.